THE MUSEUM

OF THE JEWISH
HISTORICAL
INSTITUTE

THE MUSEUM

OF THE JEWISH
HISTORICAL
INSTITUTE

Arts and Crafts

AURIGA
WYDAWNICTWA ARTYSTYCZNE I FILMOWE
Warszawa 1995

INTRODUCTION
Renata Piątkowska and Magdalena Sieramska

CATALOGUE:
CRAFTS
Iwona Brzewska and Magdalena Sieramska

PAINTING SCULPTURE GRAPHIC ART
Renata Piątkowska and Katarzyna Połujan

GRAPHIC DESIGN
Anna Tworkowska-Barankiewicz

PHOTOGRAPHS
Jan Fleischmann

Translated from the Polish
by *Bogna Piotrowska*

The book is sponsored
by Fundacja Kultury and Ministerstwo Kultury i Sztuki

ISBN 83-221-064-2-4

Text set by: WOMIK–Wojtasiak, Warszawa
Colour separation: PROTEA-GRAF, Warszawa
Printed and bound in Poland by DEKA, Kraków

INTRODUCTION

he idea of forming a Jewish museum first arose in 1944 in Lublin, shortly after the town had been liberated from the German occupation. The task of collecting and preserving the heritage – or rather its minute part that had escaped annihilation during the war – of Polish and European Jewry was entrusted to the Jewish Historical Commission acting on behalf of the Central Committee of Jews in Poland, which on 28 December 1944 adopted the name of the Central Jewish Historical Commission. In March 1945 the Commission was transferred from Lublin to Łódź and soon it established local branches all over Poland.[1]

In its report for the period of 15 December 1944 to 30 April 1945,[2] the Commission recognized as one of its main tasks the opening of a museum. The aim of this museum, according to its organizers, was to carry on the work of pre-war collections in museums and private hands, which had been destroyed and broken up during the German occupation. However some time had to elapse before the idea could be put into practice.

In the autumn of 1947, following a decision of the Central Committee of Jews in Poland, the Central Historical Commission was transformed into a Jewish Historical Institute (ŻIH) and moved to Warsaw to the reconstructed building in 5 Tłomackie street which before the war had housed the Main Jewish Library and the Institute of Judaic Sciences This is where the archives, library and museum collections which the Commission had amassed in the meantime had been deposited. The Museum, operating as part of the Institute, formally began its activity on 19 April 1948, the fifth anniversary of the uprising in the Jewish ghetto in Warsaw, with the ceremonious opening of two exhibitions: "The Martyrdom and Struggle of Polish Jews in 1939–45" and "A Gallery of Paintings by Jewish Artists Murdered by the German Invaders".[3] In post-war Poland, this was the first museum to collect and popularize the centuries-long

---

[1] *35 lat działalności Żydowskiego Instytutu Historycznego w Polsce Ludowej* (36 years of the activity of the Jewish Historical Institute in People's Poland), Warszawa 1980, pp. 7–8.

[2] Archives of the Jewish Historical Institute (hereinafter referred to as ŻIH Archives), Correspondence for 1944.

[3] *35 lat...*, op. cit., p. 15.

cultural heritage of the Jewish people and to commemorate the struggle and martyrdom of Jews during the Second World War.

The Jewish Historical Institute, through its branches all over Poland, continued tracing mementoes of the Jewish past. The museum collections were enlarged with new purchases, gifts and deposits. New exhibits flowed in from the sites of former ghettos, above all those in Łódź and Warsaw, from former extermination camps and German collections of Judaica. The largest number of such collections were discovered in Lower Silesia, close to the Polish-Czechoslovakian border (e.g. the Kłodzko region). This was where the Germans had sent various objects representing the cultural heritage of the people condemned to extermination. Some of those objects they had destroyed or sold, some they had taken to Prague where they had planned to form a Jewish museum serving Nazi propaganda. The rest found its way to the Jewish Museum in Warsaw.

The museum collection was expanded considerably as a result of several major transfers.

In June 1949 the Municipal Museum in Toruń donated to the Institute several dozen objects consisting of ritual silverware and fabrics. These constituted the heritage of Jews from the Chełmno area and had been stored by the Germans in the Toruń museum.

In October of the same year, following a resolution of the Central Committee of Jews in Poland, the collections of the Jewish Society for Promoting the Fine Arts in Poland were transferred to the Jewish Institute and the Society was dissolved. In this way the Museum acquired several hundred works of art which had been collected by the Society and purchased from funds provided by the Central Committee of Jews in Poland in 1946–49.

On winding up its activity in Poland in 1950, Joint (the American Jewish Joint Distribution Committee) donated to the Museum over a hundred objects, including ritual vessels (silverware), textiles and paintings.

On three occasions the Museum enlarged its collections thanks to the Ministry of Culture and Art: in 1949, with a gift of paintings by Jan Gotard, Eliasz Kanarek, Dawid Greinfenberg and Efraim and Menasze Seidenbeutel, which had been shown in London in 1939 at an exhibition of the Blok Union of the Polish Artists; in 1951 with a transfer of 150 synagogal objects until then kept in the Narożno Castle in Bożkowo and in 1967, with a donation of 25 paintings which commemorated the tenth anniversary of the uprising in the Warsaw ghetto.

The major part of the present collection was amassed in the late 1940's and early 1950's. Later on new exhibits were acquired through gifts and bequests and to a much lesser extent through purchases, owing to the Institute's meagre financial resources.[4]

---

[4] Funds for the activity of the Jewish Historical Institute were provided until 1950 by the Central Committee of Jews in Poland, after its liquidation until 1952 by the Ministry of Higher Education, and since then until today by the Polish Academy of Sciences. Until 1968 it also occasionally obtained assistance from Joint through the Central Jewish Welfare Commission.

The Museum of the Jewish Historical Institute is divided into three departments, dealing respectively with: painting, engravings and sculpture; religious objects used in both synagogal and domestic ceremonies; and historic mementoes, mainly objects pertaining to the struggle and martyrdom of the Jewish people during the Second World War.

The largest of these is the first group, which surpasses the religious collection both in quantity and quality. The major part of this collection is composed of works by Jewish artists, the earliest dating from the 19th century, while the period before the Second World War is particularly well represented. The late appearance of Jewish painters and sculptors can be explained by two factors: first, the centuries-long isolation of Jewish culture and its resilience to European influences; and secondly, a canonical injunction contained in the second commandment of the Decalogue which says: "Thou shalt have no other gods before me. Thou shalt not make unto thee any graven image, or any likeness of any thing that is in heaven above, or that is in the earth beneath, or that is in the water under the earth" (Ex. xx, 3–4). This changed with the Haskalah, or the Jewish Enlightenment, a movement that promoted the cultural and social revival of Jews and led to their becoming acquainted with modern European culture. Between 1750 and 1880 the Haskalah spread to Germany, Italy, Western Europe and Poland.

This movement did not spurn ancient religious and cultural traditions. On the contrary, as Aleksander Hertz writes, "the followers of the Haskalah believed that Jewry – through a change in customs and a reform of ethos –would be able to free itself gradually from the tight framework of the caste structure, that it would cease to be a despised group, and it would develop the feeling of its own dignity and significance in relation to others".[5]

The Haskalah had an influence on the emergence of emancipation movements and contributed to the development of the assimilation ideology among Polish Jews: "At that time assimilation did not mean moving from one nationality group to another, it did not mean treachery or apostasy in relation to the [Jewish] people, or that this people had to be abandoned. An assimilated Jew simply passed from one cultural system to another."[6]

In Poland the first painters of Jewish origin were Aleksander Lesser (1814––84), Aleksander Sochaczewski (1843–1923) and Maurycy Gottlieb (1856–79). Since however only Gottlieb tackled Jewish themes, he came to be regarded as the father of Jewish painting in Poland. Apart from one oil painting, *Head of an Old Man,* the Museum boasts three drawn sketches by Gottlieb: *Dancing Jews, Man and Woman in the Cemetery* and *Study of a Figure,* as well as a copy of his *Self-portrait in Arab Garb* painted by Maurycy's younger brother, Marcin (1869–1936).

Maurycy Gottlieb became a model for younger Jewish artists. His followers included Maurycy Trębacz, Jakub Weinles (1870–1938), Samuel Hirszenberg,

5 A. Hertz, *Żydzi w kulturze polskiej* (Jews in Polish Culture), Paris 1961, p. 129.
6 *Ibid.,* p. 154.

Leopold Pilichowski (1864/69–1933), Natan Altman, and Zygmunt Nadel, though, unlike their predecessor, none of them engaged in heroic struggles to define their national identity. Regarding themselves as Jewish artists, they were nevertheless closely involved with Polish artistic life.

They were mainly interested in Jewish subjects and painted genre and religious pictures, historical scenes and portraits. As regards style, they were academicians, in particular Leopold Horowitz, Zygmunt Nadel and Natan Altman.

In the Museum of the Jewish Historical Institute, Leopold Pilichowski, Jakub Weinles and Natan Altman are represented by one work each, and these do not always distinctively illustrate their style. On the other hand the Museum boasts interesting retrospective collections of the work of Maurycy Trębacz, Samuel Hirszenberg and Artur Markowicz.

The earliest of Trębacz's paintings date from the 1880's and 1890's. These are mainly portraits (*Portrait of a Man, Portrait of Uncle*) and "religious" portraits (*Jew with Etrog, Jew in Tallith, Jew in Fur Hat* and one of his several versions of *Yankel's Concert*). We also have a number of his landscapes painted slightly later (*Kazimierz on the Vistula, Cottage at the Foot of Wawel Hill*). In addition, the Museum collection includes the artist's personal archives, discovered in the Łódź ghetto, which contains letters, family photos, sketches, reproductions of works and some oil sketches. Although he tackled various subjects, Trębacz is regarded as a Jewish painter first and foremost.

Samuel Hirszenberg, too, is best known thanks to his works on Jewish religious life (*Anathema, Jews in Prayer, Interior of a Synagogue*). Apart from numerous drawings, oil sketches and pastels on Jewish themes, the Museum has in its collections his marvellous impressionistic landscapes (*Landscape with a Girl, Rural Landscape in Winter*) and symbolic canvases (*The Artist and His Muse*).

The 600 drawings, pastels and oils by Artur Markowicz form the largest collection of works by a single artist, large enough in fact for us to trace the development of his talent and study his style in detail. The finest works are undoubtedly landscapes of Belgium, Zakopane, Gorlice and Cracow, and pastels on the everyday life and festivals of Jews. We also have several fine portraits of the artist's wife, self-portraits and portrait studies.

The "ethnographic" current inaugurated by these artists was carried on in 1918–39 by Adolf Messer (*In the Synagogue, Seder*), Mojżesz Rynecki, Leon Lewkowicz (*Jew with a Pipe*) and Maks Haneman (*Jewish Tailor*).

In the early 20th century younger artists, Leopold Gottlieb (Maurycy's brother) and Wilhelm Wachtel, came under the influence of Art Nouveau. Our best known work dating from that period is Leopold Gottlieb's *Portrait of Dr. Ber Kupczyk*. A soft Art Nouveau style appears in the work of Wachtel, e.g. *Study of a Jewish Boy,* and the lithographic portfolio entitled *Farewell to Golus,* and in Jerzy Merkel's early work, *Portrait of a Man*, which was discernibly influenced by Stanisław Wyspiański.

The earliest sculptures in our collection date from the Young Poland (Art Nouveau) period: Konstanty Laszczka's *Head of a Jew*, Henryk Glicenstein's *Messiah,* works by Józef Mojżesz Gabowicz (1862–1939), and *Head of a Smiling Girl* by Ber Szymon Kratka (1885–1960) which was later reproduced in a slightly different version by Abraham Ostrzega (1899–1942).

Adolf Edward Herstein (1869–1932), a graphic artist and painter who worked and taught in his own studio in Warsaw and Berlin, was on the whole an impressionist (*In the Yoke*). His contemporary, the graphic artist Adam Herszaft, was the author of lyrical female portraits and landscapes, mostly of Italy (*Sicily, Old Walls, Trees*).

Although as early as the 19th century Jewish artists constituted a fairly numerous group, they failed to produce a separate artistic tradition and their style followed closely contemporary currents. It was only after the First World War that a distinct Polish-Jewish artistic milieu emerged. This was very numerous and fairly well organized (the Jewish Society for the Promotion of the Fine Arts and the Association of Jewish Artists in Poland); hence the major part of the collection of the Jewish Historical Institute dates from the twenty years between the wars.

The Jewish artistic milieu in Poland was very diversified. Only artists associated with the journal "Yung Yiddish" – Vincent Brauner, Henryk Barciński, Mojżesz Broderson, Jankiel Adler and Marek Szwarc – attempted to create a new Jewish artistic tradition. According to J. Malinowski, the Yung Yiddish group "seems to be the only significant purely Jewish artistic group which consciously underlined its belonging to Yiddish culture".[7] Its members, inspired by the work of Marc Chagall, Ludwig Meidner, Oskar Kokoschka and Isaac Ryback – belonged to a separate current referred to as "Jewish Expressionism".

Not many works by Yung Yiddish artists have come down to us. The library of the Jewish Historical Institute has in its collection issues nos. 2–3 and 4–6 of the journal "Jung Idysz", as well as volumes of poetry by Mojżesz Broderson (1890–1956), entitled *Cungelungen, Sznej tanc*, both with covers designed by the poet, and *Perły na bruku* (Pearls on the pavement) with illustrations by Józef Hecht (1891–1952), and Abraham Zak's book *Pod skrzydłami śmierci* (Under the Wings of Death) with its cover and illustrations designed by Jankiel Adler (1895–1949).

As well as this, we have works by members of this group dating from either the earlier (Brauner) or later period (Henryk Barciński's *Legless Beggar on a Wheel Cart, Sitting Man, The Sacrifice of Isaac,* 1932, *Head of a Girl*).

Metalwork has been generally regarded as a traditionally Jewish technique, which attracted many artists, including those from the Yung Ydish circle, e.g. Vincent Brauner (*Water Carrier,* 1929) and Marek Szwarc. Some artists devoted themselves entirely to copperwork, for example Joachim Kahane and

7 J. Malinowski, *Grupa "Jung Idysz" i żydowskie środowisko "Nowej Sztuki" w Polsce 1918–1923* (The "Yung Yiddish" group and the Jewish milieu of "New Art" in Poland in 1918–23), Warszawa 1987, p. 13.

Henryk Chaimowicz (1895–1940/43) who produced mostly portraits and more rarely genre scenes. Metalwork was also the favourite medium of some artists who made their début in the 1930's, e.g. Arie Merzer (1905–66), Chaim Hanft (1899–1951) and Chaim Goldberg (1917).

In the work of many artists Jewish themes receded into the background and appeared only sporadically, mostly as genre scenes in landscape settings, e.g. in Maks Haneman and Ernö Erb. Purely technical concerns – the search for colour schemes and texture – became more important, and the favourite genres were landscape and still-life.

Throughout the twenty years between the wars, the realistic tradition prevailed in both genre and landscape painting. The impressionist influence could be discerned in composition and colour scheme, e.g. Marcin Kitz, Maks Haneman, Leon Rozenblum, Henryk Rabinowicz, Natan Korzeń and Abraham Neuman. Post-impressionist tendencies appeared in the work of Ernö Erb, Roman Rozental (1897–1942), Symche Trachter and Adolf Behrmann and, in the 1930's, colouristic elements in the work of Emil Szinagel, Henryk Cytryn and Dawid Greifenberg.

Jewish artists were members of almost all artistic groups active in the inter-war period. Even before the First World War Artur Markowicz belonged to the "Sztuka" Society of Polish Artists. Henryk Gotlib came under the influence of Formism, a Polish variety of Expressionism. The "Rytm" Association of Polish Artists had among its members Roman Kramsztyk, Henryk Kuna, Eugeniusz Zak (1884–1926) and Leopold Gottlieb, while Henryk Berlewi was one of the founders of the "Blok" group.

Tadeusz Pruszkowski's pupils in the Warsaw Academy of Fine Arts included Jan Gotard and Eliasz Kanarek, both members of the St. Luke Fraternity, Efraim and Menasze Seidenbeutel from the "Szkoła Warszawska" Association and Gizela Hufnagel.

Only the Seidenbeutels' collection may be regarded as a representative sample of work. The Museum has 17 paintings by the two brothers dating from various periods: *View from the Window*, *Boy with a Fishing Rod*, *Wayside Poplars*, *Marina*, *Landscape from Cieszyn Silesia*, *Mulatto Girl*, *Portrait of a Man Wearing a Hat*, *Still-life*, two versions of *A View of Kazimierz on the Vistula*, and others.

The Jewish painter Norbert Strassberg was a member of the "Horned Heart Tribe" formed by Stanisław Szukalski.

The following were members of avant-garde groups active in the 1930's: Otto Hahn (1904–42), Marek Włodarski, Ludwik Lille (1897–1957) and Aleksander Riemer (1880–1943) who all belonged to "artes" of Lvov, and Berta Grünberg, Sasza Blonder and Karol and Szymon Piasecki associated with the Grupa Krakowska.

The work of artists from the "Phrygian Cap" group is represented by Chaim Hanft and Józef Herman (1912).

Jewish artists active in Łódź formed a large and vigorous community.
This group is represented in the Museum by Natan Szpigel, Ignacy Hirsz-

fang and a large collection of works (44) by Samuel Finkelstein. All the artists mentioned above were associated with the "Start" Society of Artists and Friends of the Fine Arts. Another Łódź artist was Adolf Behrmann, author of portraits and landscapes, mostly eastern, many of which are now in our Museum.

The collection of sculpture is rather small and haphazard. Portraits prevail, including several anonymous heads in wood representing characteristic Jewish types. The majority of objects date from the 1920's and 1930's: Roman Kramsztyk's *Head of a Woman Wearing a Turban,* Henryk Kuna's *Bust of Felicja Winawer,* Magdalena Gross' *Female Head* and *Male Head*, and Helena Głogowska's *Motherhood*. Only Józef Mojżesz Gabowicz and Ryszard Moszkowski are represented by a larger number of works.

Few sculptures in our possession date from the post-war period. The most valuable of these is the plaster relief of the scene from the back wall of the monument to the Heroes of the Ghetto by Natan Rappaport (1911–87), as well as compositions dedicated to the struggle in the Warsaw ghetto: *The Fighting Ghetto* by Alina Szapocznikow (1926–73) and *The Fighters of the Warsaw Ghetto* by Romuald Gruszczyński.

As regards quality the collection of graphic art and drawings is inferior to the painting and sculpture collections. As is the case with painting, scenes of Jewish life predominate, e.g. in the drawings by Samuel Hirszenberg and Artur Markowicz, the series of lithographs of the *Old Jewish Life* by Hersz Danielewicz (Harry Daniels), lithographs by Maks Eliowicz, Rachela Marcus-Szalit and Jan Feliks Piwarski, and illustrations to Eliza Orzeszkowa's novel *Meir Ezofowicz* by Michał E. Andriolli.

In the inter-war years some graphic artists were interested mostly in landscape and portraiture. The Museum boasts works by Fiszel Zylberberg, Natalia Landau's (1907–43) *Cottage,* Mojżesz Gurewicz's (1905–43/44) *Mountain Landscape* and *Landscape with a Road,* as well as two coloured woodcuts, *The Old Town* and *A View of Okólnik Street from St. Casimir's Convent,* by Aniela Cukierówna, one of the most original artists in the 1930's.

Bruno Schulz occupies a special position in the history of Polish art. The Museum has six drawings by this artist, besides those that are reproduced in this book the *Self-portrait,* 1919, and *Playful Women,* 1916.

The museum collections include few works by artists from outside Poland, mostly prints and drawings. Germany is particularly well represented with works by Max Liebermann (*Self-portrait, Portrait of Hermann Cohen*), Emil Orlik, Lesser Ury (1861–1931), Jozef Israëls (1824–1911) and Alexander Oppler (1869–1937). The showpiece of this collection are the etchings by Josef Budko: illustrations to the *Passover Haggadah* and landscapes from the area of Płońsk. We also have individual prints by Hermann Struck, Leo Peysak (1894–?) and Hugo Krayn (1885–1919).

There is no room here to list the work of all artists represented in the Museum of the Jewish Historical Institute. Let us, however, mention some more names, since frequently the only trace left of their existence is a painting or a print rescued from the war and preserved in our Museum.

We know little of the life and work of Julia Acker (1898–1942), Józef Badower, Henryk Epstein (1892–1944), Arie Leon Fein (1906), Feliks Frydman, the brothers Aron (1913–39) and Tobiasz Haber (1906–43), Ber Horowitz (1895–1941), a poet and a painter, Jakub Merkiel (1912–?), Abraham Michałowicz (c. 1900–40/44), Marceli Słodki (1892–1943), Józef Mitler, Hersz Weber (1903/4–42), Bencion Cukierman (1890/95–1942/44) and Pinkas Zelman (1907–36).

The Second World War cut short the magnificently developing work of many Jewish artists. The majority of them perished in ghettos and extermination camps, few survived the inferno of the concentration camps or managed to hide on the Arian side. Many paid with their lives for attempting to escape from the ghetto – Jan Gotard and Julia Ringel-Keilowa were killed on the streets of Warsaw. Some could not endure the hardship of hiding – Aniela Cukierówna died of exhaustion shortly before the outbreak of the Warsaw uprising in 1944; Magdalena Gross and Henryk Kuna died shortly after the war.

Many artists continued their work in ghettos and camps. Their work constitutes an invaluable document of the martyrdom of the Jewish people.

Watercolours and drawings by Gela Seksztajn were hidden in Ringelblum's Archives. Certain drawings by Lewinson and lithographs by Krzysztof Henisz (1914–78) were made in the Warsaw ghetto. More works were preserved in the Łódź ghetto: metalwork and water colours by Vincent Brauner, sanguines by Natan Szpigel, pastels by Izrael Lejzerowicz, watercolours by Józef Kowner (1895/1902–67), paintings by Sara Gliksman (1910) and Hersz Szyllis.

In the cellars in the city centre, where after the Warsaw uprising Dr. Henryk Beck and his wife hid, he painted the series entitled *Bunker 1944*.[8]

The period immediately after the war saw the appearance of works by Jonasz Stern (1904–88; *Deportation of Children*, *Street in the Lvov Ghetto*), Marek Włodarski (1903–60; *Jewish Forced Labour*, *Before the Crematorium at Stutthof*), Abba Fenichel (1906–86) (*Prisoner*, *Jewish Family*), Leopold Lewicki (1906–73; *Ghetto*, *Bound for Bełżec*, *The Last Road*) and Henryk Hechtkopf (1910; *Ruins of the Warsaw Ghetto*). A witness of the annihilation of Lithuanian Jews was Józef Charyton (1910–75) represented in our collection by a series of 185 drawings in ink and charcoal.

The works dedicated to the uprising in the Warsaw ghetto and painted in the 1950's include: Jadwiga Mijalowa's *Fighting at Gęsia Street,* Witold Miller's *Assistance by the People's Guard,* Stanisław Żółtowski's *Revenge Air Raid by Soviet Aviators,* paintings by Zdzisław Lachur and portraits of Mordechaj Anielewicz and Józef Lewartowski by Janusz Paweł Janowski. However it was only the young artists, Izaak Celnikier (1923) and Marek Oberländer, who brought painting on the theme of martyrdom unto a high artistic level.

   [8] J. Jaworska, *Henryka Becka "Bunkier 1944"* (Henryk Beck's "Bunker 1944"), Wrocław 1982.

The section of post-war art has few really outstanding works. Mention should be made of paintings by Aron (Adam) Muszka (1914) recalling Chagall's style (*Jewish Boy, Purimspil*) and a series of lyrical views of Vilna by Rafał Chwoles. We do not have in our collection works by Jewish artists who were active after the war. Particularly painful is the lack of works by Jonasz Stern, Izaak Celnikier, Erna Rosenstein, Leopold Buczkowski and Zofia Woźna.

The religious collection is much more modest and numbers merely several hundred objects used in synagogal and domestic ceremonies, including objects in silver and other metals, textiles, Torah scrolls and illuminated Books of Esther on parchment. The majority of them date from the 19th century and only a few items come from the 18th century.

Besides objects used by the Ashkenazim which form the bulk of our collection, we have religious objects reverting to the culture and crafts of the Sephardim. These consist of ritual textiles and Torah finials – rimmonim. It seems that they were the property of Greek Jews who in 1943 perished in Auschwitz.

Apart from Polish Judaica, we have items from German centres, including Berlin, Wrocław and Lower Silesia, from Russia and from Austria.

The objects of German provenance were bequeathed by the Municipal Museum in Toruń and, as the inscriptions that have been deciphered indicate, come from synagogues in Toruń and Chełmża. Following the first partition of Poland in 1772 these cities became part of Prussia, hence the influx of German Jews to these areas. This was a small but wealthy community[9] – as can be deduced from the silverware and fabrics which have been preserved – remaining in close contact with the Jewish communities in other German towns, notably Berlin and Frankfurt on Main.

Religious objects for the needs of the Jewish population were produced by both Jewish and Christian craftsmen.

The socio-political status of European Jews, which remained unstable in fact until the mid-19th century, and the rigid rules of the guild system hampered the development of Jewish craftsmanship and had an adverse effect on its standards. To ply their trade Jewish craftsmen needed a special individual permission and only then were they allowed to form Jewish guilds, which provided competition for their Christian counterparts (in the 18th century such guilds were widespread in particular in Eastern Europe, in Poland and Moravia). Otherwise they had to work illegally, outside the guild system.

This situation is reflected in objects of silverwork brought together in the Museum. Earlier items, dating from the late 18th and early 19th centuries, are as a rule unsigned. In such cases it is only through comparison that we can define approximately the provenance of an object. Frequently, as the place of origin, we give a general area, e.g. Eastern Europe, where certain characteristic features as regards ornaments and workmanship prevailed. The marks of individual

---

[9] E.g., in Toruń there were 426 Jews in 1846, and 1,020 in 1910. From: *Dzieje Torunia* (History of Toruń), Toruń 1933, p. 245.

silversmiths are encountered only on later objects, dating from the end of the first half of the 19th century. These were the so-called consensus silversmiths who by buying a patent acquired complete freedom to pursue their trade.

The collection of the Jewish Historical Institute boasts a particularly large number of objects produced by Warsaw silversmiths, including Hersz Szyldberg, Jankiel Kelmer, Szmul Szkarłat, M. Charłap and Abraham Reiner, as well as such Christian craftsmen as Jan Pogorzelski, Karol Filip Malcz and Antoni Riedel.

Beginning in the second half of the 19th century, the needs of the three million strong Jewish community in Poland were also satisfied by industry. Examples of cheap, mass-produced objects in the Museum include silver-plated hanukkah lamps, spice boxes and candlesticks produced by Norblin, Fraget, B. Buch, Handelsman and Zylberberg.

Berlin silverwork is represented by Joachim Hübner (1737 – mentioned for the last time in 1778) and Johann August Gebhardt (1790–1860), Wrocław by Georg Kahlert the Younger, and Russia by Pavel Sazikov (his company was established in 1793).

The form of the objects in silver and other metals is a combination of various historical styles, folk motifs and traditional religious symbols. Their frequently traditional style is a result of the customers' attachment to old, established patterns. This is true, for example, of Torah shields (in classical baroque style) produced by Berlin goldsmiths in the first half of the 19th century (one of them was the above-mentioned J. A. Gebhardt) which were modelled on shields produced by the goldsmith Ludwig Christian Bartelles (1786–1804) active in the city of Celle near Berlin, as well as of spice boxes dating from 1921–30 which faithfully imitate 19th century filigree work.

The 19th century witnessed a return to historical styles. In the silverware in the possession of the Museum we can discern traces of late Renaissance ornaments, e.g. in Malcz's spice boxes, rococo elements in a pair of candlesticks originating probably in Silesia (the so-called second rococo), classical motifs in J. Pogorzelski's candlesticks. However baroque elements predominate since neo-baroque ruled supreme in the second half of the 19th century.

The majority of objects in silver and other metals represent a high artistic level and they come from such important centres as Warsaw, Berlin, Wrocław, Vienna, Moscow, Kiev and Jerusalem.

A separate group is formed by a collection of Sephardic rimmonim dating from the late 19th and early 20th centuries. All of them are in the shape of pomegranates, in gilded repoussé or stamped metal, and are of mediocre artistic level. Their ornaments are a mixture of eastern motifs with elements of European, notably baroque, art.

The collection of ritual objects in metal is not large and comprises brass candlesticks and hanukkah lamps dating for the most part from the 19th–20th centuries, with only some incomplete pieces which probably originated in the late 18th and early 19th centuries in Eastern Europe. The openwork backs of the brass hanukkah lamps in particular, as is the case with the illuminated Megillat Esther, demonstrate folk art motifs; their line is occasionally reminiscent of Jewish paper cuts with which houses were decorated on the festival of Shavout.

A separate group is made up of several brass Bezalel objects, inlaid with silver and copper (so-called Damascene workmanship) dating from 1906–26. The objects in question consist of decorative festival plates and a vase.

The Museum boasts Poland's largest collection of Jewish religious fabrics (over a hundred pieces), used both in the synagogue: aron ha-kodesh curtains, Torah mantles, tablecloths (to cover the bimah and the cantor's pulpit), Torah binders, wedding canopies; and in domestic ceremonies: festival tablecloths, matzah bags, bags for tephilin and tallith, and prayer shawls (talliths and atarahs).

The oldest of them – five parokhets and two Torah binders – go back to the 18th century, while the rest date from the 19th and 20th centuries.

Some of them, especially the oldest items, represent a high level of craftsmanship and were evidently produced to special orders in well-known workshops. Later objects, dating from the 19th century, are frequently mass-produced, with some established patterns recurring. A large group is made up of items woven, sewn and embroidered by women from fabrics originally meant for secular purposes (for example, items which had once served as garments, upholstery, etc.). Various recognized rabbinical authorities allowed for such practices.

It is difficult to ascertain which workshops individual pieces came from. Some of the fabrics which were donated by the Toruń museum were produced in Germany, most probably in Prussia. Considering that Jews who settled in the area of Chełmno were in close touch with Berlin and Frankfurt on Main, we may assume that many such items came from one of the two towns. It is known that the Jewish community in Berlin established textile works in Pomerania and that in the area on the Noteć river, which as a result of the first partition of Poland became part of Prussia, textile workshops employing mainly women were in operation.

Sephardic textiles in the Museum collection are mostly made from "second-hand" fabrics. The most impressive of them are fabrics embroidered in rich gold and silver eastern patterns. Compared with Ashkenazi fabrics, they are characterized by a more abundant floral and plant ornamentation or birds and less typical religious symbols; the most frequent motifs are a crown and the Star of David.

Religious textiles of Polish provenance are few, and establishing their place of origin is usually impossible, with the exception of a collection of atarahs in metal thread: some of the atarahs may have come from Sasowo (now in the Ukraine), the town which was once famous in this field.

The most precious of the manuscripts in the collection are illuminated scrolls of the Book of Esther written on parchment. There are seven illuminated manuscripts, dated to the 18th–19th centuries, and one ornamented with 15 copper-plate illustrations. They come from Poland, Italy, the Netherlands and Bohemia.

Objects for synagogal and domestic worship feature traditional themes and symbols with their roots in the Old Testament, Talmud and Zohar.[10] Although the second commandment was a hindrance, severe religious injunctions were not strictly adhered to and even figural scenes appeared. It should be remembered that the prohibition against depicting what is on the earth, in the air and in the water was closely related to the ban on worshipping false idols, which could be variously interpreted, a fact which made it easier for Jewish crafts to develop. The Museum of the Jewish Historical Institute has in its collection a Torah shield with likenesses of Moses and Aaron and a parokhet with the scene of Abraham's sacrifice, both dating from the 18th century. Craftsmen also took recourse to biblical flora and fauna enriched with elements of native scenery. In the case of objects for synagogal worship in the Museum, the most popular, typically Jewish motifs include: a crown, the Star of David, compositions with two lions supporting the tablet of the Decalogue or a menorah, elements of the aron ha-kodesh with columns (in commemoration of the two columns in the Temple of Solomon named after Jachin and Boaz), eagles, doves, peacocks, stags, lions, fish, palm trees, vines, grapes, pomegranates, olive blossoms and fruit, acorns and oak branches. These motifs are usually arranged antithetically and as a rule their meaning is complex and ambiguous. The key to their interpretation should be sought in the above-mentioned holy books and universal symbolism.

The items in the possession of the Museum of the Jewish Historical Institute constitute only a tiny part of the long lasting heritage of the people who once lived in large numbers in this part of Europe. We hope that this book and the collection presented in it will bring closer to the readers the world of those Jews whom fate had for centuries linked with Poles.

Finally we wish to express our heartfelt gratitude to all those who with their valuable remarks helped us in compiling this album, notably to Dr. Shifra Epstein, professor at the University of Texas, and Mr. Zusi Efron, the retired director of the Museum of Art in the Ein Harod kibutz.

Renata Piątkowska and Magdalena Sieramska

---

[10] The Book of Splendour, the main work of Jewish mystical literature, so-called Kabbalah, dating from the 13th century.

CATALOGUE

1. Torah shield, Poland, 18th cent.
Silver, repoussé, 20.3 × 16.1 cm.
Inv. no. C-212 / Purchased in 1948.

2. Torah shield, Wrocław, 18th cent.
Silver, repoussé, cast, engraved, gilded, set with rock crystal and opals in cassette mounting with ruff, 34.2 × 28.5 cm.
Signed: (1) city mark of Wrocław: head of St. John on a bowl; (2) goldsmith's initials "CAW" in an irregular oval (letter "A" without the horizontal bar).
Inv. no. C-209 / Donated by Joint in 1950.

3. Torah shield, Berlin, first quarter of the 19th cent., Monogrammist "GWH"
Silver, repoussé, cast, engraved and gilded, 37 × 32 cm.
Signed: (1) city mark of Berlin: a bear in an oval with letter "I" to the right; (2) goldsmith's initials "GWH" in a rectangle; (3) assay zigzag.
Inv. no. C-217 / Donated by the Municipal Museum in Toruń in 1949.
Dedicatory inscription: נדר לבה״כנ מאיר גורמאן זצ״ל
"Offering to the synagogue by p[ious] Meir Gurman [of] b[lessed] m[emory]".

4. Torah shield, Wrocław, 1762–72, Georg Kahlert (the Younger), 1732–1772
Silver, repoussé, cast and gilded, 36 × 30 cm.
Signed: (1) city mark of Wrocław: head of St. John on a bowl; (2) silversmith's mark: initials "GK" in a rectangle with convex corners, with a star between the letters; (3) date letter "G" in a circle (1761–76); (4) Prussian free state mark from 1809; (5) assay zigzag.
Inv. no. C-216 / Donated by Joint in 1950.
Inscription in the central cartouche:
ממונים אמונים על משמר / הבית המקדש מעט האהלופי
הגבאי ר״בה״כ ק״ק לבוב פה ברעסל״ה ליפמן בר״מ
והמיכאל ס״ר ישראל מ״ל אשר הותירו במשמרתם
לקנות כלי הקדש זה לפרט ויצף אהם זהב / לפק
Chosen to ... guard the small shrine
chief aluph gabbai chairman of the synagogue
of the sacred community of Lvov (here in Wrocław)? Lipman son of the rabbi teacher and Michael ... Israel ...
who left this liturgical object purchased during their holy service.
According to the date: "... overlaid them with gold" (Ex. xxxvii, [5]533 (=1773).
Inscription in the right and left cartouche:
לפרט / ויּשׁב / יעֲקֹב / בּארץ / מגּוֹרי / אבֹיו / לפק
According to the date: "Jacob dwelt in the land wherein his father was a stranger..." (Gen. xxxvii, 1) [5]522 (=1762).
(The date is the sum of the numerical values denoted by the dots of the letters).

5. Torah shield, Płock?, 1857, Monogrammist "MZ"
Silver, repoussé, cast and engraved, filigree, 23 × 18.4 cm.
Signed: (1) goldsmith's mark: initials "MZ" in italics in a square; (2) device of the workshop: lion passant in an oval.
Inv. no. C-300 / Purchased in 1985.
Inscription on the door: ויהי בנסוע / הארון / ויאמר משה

"When the ark set forward ... Moses said... (Num. x, 35).
Below, the tablets of the Decalogue and a cartouche supported by two stags with the inscription: פה פלאצק / שנת / תריז לפק
"Płock [5]617"(=1857).
On the column bases, the names of the columns from the temple of Solomon: בעז (Boaz), and יכין (Jachin) (1 Kings vii, 21; 2 Chron. iii, 17). In the lower section, the donor's name: יצחק (Isaac).

6. Torah shield, Berlin, second half of the 19th cent., Monogrammist "F.eC."
Silver, repoussé, cast, engraved and gilded, 35.7 × 29.7 cm.
Signed: (1) city mark of Berlin: a bear in a circle with date letter "K" to the right; (2) goldsmith's initials "F.eC."; (3) letter "C" in a circle: (4) assay zigzag.
Inv. no. C-218 / Donated by the Municipal Museum in Toruń in 1949.

7. Torah shield, Germany?, 19th cent.
Silvered repoussé metal, cast and gilded, 34.5 × 26 cm.
Inv. no. C-217 / Found in the Łódź ghetto, in the ŻIH Museum since 1947.

8. Torah shield, Germany, 1893
Silver, repoussé, cast, engraved and gilded, 30.5 × 24.2 cm.
Signed: (1) Prussian state hallmark: crescent, crown, standard "800"; (2) undecipherable workshop device.
Inv. no. C-223 / Found in the Łódź ghetto, in the ŻIH Museum since 1947.
Inscription: ב״ר שמואל זצ״ל אלכסנדר ליפשיטץ
בת״ר אברהם יוסף זצ״ל ז״ג טשארנע גלאטצער
ת״ר שנת נ״ג ל
"S[on of the] p[ious] r[abbi] Samuel [of] b[lessed] m[emory] Aleksander Lipszyc / Daughter [of the] p[ious] r[abbi] Abraham Józef [of] b[lessed] m[emory] .... Czarna Glotzer / Year [5]653" (=1893).

9. Torah crown, Berlin, late 19th cent.
Silver, punched, cast, engraved and gilded, 34 × 14 cm.
Signed: (1) city mark of Berlin: a bear in an oval with letter "M" to the right; (2) letter "M"; (3) unidentified device (goldsmith's mark?) in an oval.
Inv. no. C-225 / Donated by the Municipal Museum in Toruń in 1949.

10. Torah crown, Poland, 1853
Silver, punched, cast and gilded, 26.5 × 19 cm.
Signed: (1) goldsmith's name "A. Icek" in italics in a rectangle; (2) standard "12" in a square; (3) undecipherable name "...erin" (Szterin?) in italics in a rectangle.
Inv. no. C-232 / Donated by Joint in 1950.
Dedicatory inscription:
זה הכתר שייך להחברה קדושה מקק, קראשניק שנת תריג לפק
"The Crown of the Burial Society of the s[acred] c[ommunity] of Kraśnik Year [5]613" (=1853).

11. Rimmon, Germany?, late 19th cent.
Metal, cast, punched, silvered and gilded, 44.5 cm.
Inv. no. C-230 / Donated by CKHwŁ in 1947.

12. Rimmon, Greece, 19th cent.
Silver, filigree, 22.5 cm.
Inv. no. C-307 / Donated by MKiS* in 1951.

13. Rimmonim, Greece, 19th/20th cent.
Metal, repoussé, engraved and silvered, 27 cm.
Inv. no. C-330 / Donated by MKiS in 1951.

---
* MKiS = the Ministry of Culture and Art.

14. Rimmonim, Salonika, 19th/20th cent.
Metal, repoussé, silvered and engraved, 31.5 cm.
Inv. no. C-331 / Donated by MKiS in 1951.

15. Rimmonim, Greece, 19th/20th cent.
Metal, cast, punched, silvered and engraved, 24.5 cm.
Inv. no. C-328 / Donated by MKiS in 1951.
Dedicatory inscription:

הקדש הכובוה כה״ר אברהם פיניאל נ״ע לק״ק איבורה יע״א

"Pious ... V[enerable] R[abbi] Abraham Finyal [may his] s[hould be in]
p[aradise] f[or the] s[acred] c[ommunity of] Évora M[ay the] S[upreme
preserve you] A[men]."
Évora was the Jewish district in Salonika, as well as being the name of
a synagogue situated there.

16. Torah pointer. Poland?, first half of the 19th cent.
Silver, cast, engraved, 28.5 cm.
Signed: (1) standard "12" in a square; (2) assay groove; (3) obliterated
marks on the palm.
Inv. no. C-141 / Donated by CKŻwP branch in Katowice in 1949, probably
coming from the synagogue in Rybnik.

17. Torah pointer, late 19th cent.
Silver, punched, cast, engraved, with traces of gilding, 35 cm.
Inv. no. C-146 / Donated by CKHwŁ in 1947.

18. Torah pointer, Poland?, 19th/20th cent.
Silver, punched, cast, engraved and gilded: wood painted dark brown to
recall mahogany, buffalo horn, mother of pearl, 40.8 cm.
Standard "800".
Inv. no. C-321 / Purchased in 1988.

19. Torah pointer, Greece, 1932
Metal, cast, engraved and silvered, 38.7 cm.
Inv. no. B-509 / Donated by MKiS in 1951.
Dedicatory inscription:

תשרי | הקדש די זיולי יוסיף חאגואל

"Dedicated by dear Józef Haguel"
Inscription on the hand: שדי   "Shaddai" (Almighty).

20. Torah pointer, Łódź, 1913
Buffalo horn, wood, plastic, 29 cm.
Inv. no. C-140 / Donated by CKHwŁ in 1947.
Dedicatory inscription:

זאת נדר /אברהם יהודה בן יוסף נ״י / ת״רעיג לאדז

"Gift of Abraham Jehuda son of Joseph long may he live 1913 Łódź".

21. Torah pointer, Poland?, 19th/20th cent.
Silver, punched, cast, engraved and gilden, 26.5 cm.
Inv. no. C-142 / Donated by CKHwŁ in 1947.
Inscription: donor's name   יוסף שאבשעוויץ   ("Józef Szabszewicz").

22. Torah pointer, early 19th cent.?
Silver, repoussé, cast and engraved, 25.5 cm.
Signed: (1) letter "B" in a rectangle with its upper and lower sides oval;
(2) two undecipherable devices.
Inv. no. C-150 / Donated by CKŻwP branch in Katowice in 1948.

23. Torah pointer, Berlin?, late 19th cent.
Silver, punched, cast and engraved, 26 cm.
Signed: on the palm obliterated letter "B"?
Inv. no. C-151 / Donated by the Municipal Museum in Toruń in 1949.
Dedicatory inscription:
"Gewidmet von den Latteschen Eheleuten" (Dedicated by the Latteschs').

24. Torah pointer, Berlin?, 1866
Silver, cast, punched and engraved, 29.5 cm.
Signed: obliterated devices, on the palm, perhaps the city mark of Berlin.
Inv. no. C-148 / Donated by the Municipal Museum in Toruń in 1949.
Dedicatory inscription: מצבת היד וזאת התרומה אשר נדבה רוח בעלי מתעסקים
דקק טהאראן לספר תורה שלהם שנת כֹּתֹרֹו לפק
"This is a representation of the hand. This is an offering which is a gift of
the heart of the men in charge of the sacred community of Toruń for their
book of the Torah. [5] 626" (=1866)

25. Torah binder, Germany?, 1754
Linen embroidered in coloured silk thread, 18 × 280 cm.
Inv. no. C-85/1 / Donated by MKiS in 1951.
Sewn from four strips of linen, with, along its length, the following
inscription: [מ]שה בן כהרר שמען שליט /בוטניס/ נולד במזל
פורים תקיד לפק ה יגדלהו לתורה ולחופה ולמעשים
טובי [ם] אס

"[M]oshe son [of] v[enerable] M[aster] R[abbi]
Simon Shalit (Botnisa) born u[nder]
[the] l[ucky] s[tar] of Purim [5]514 [=1754]
may G[od make him] grow for Torah
for huppah and ma'asim tovim A[men] S[elah]."

On the second strip, under the letters, two fishes, the boy's sign of the
zodiac, with the following inscriptions at the sides: מזל דגים
"constellation of fish"
On the third strip, an unrolled Torah scroll, adorned with flower garlands
and topped with a crown, bearing the inscription:
תורה   "Torah"
משה   "Moses"
אמת   "Truth"
Under the crown: כתר תורה   "The Crown of the Torah"
The last strip features a representation of the newly-weds under the huppah
emblazoned with the following inscription:
מזל-טוב   "To luck", and beneath it
הרי את מקודשת לי   [With this ring] you are hallowed to me*.

* The formula pronounced by the bridegroom when he gives the ring to his bride.

26. Torah binder, Germany?, 1861
Linen, inscriptions and ornaments painted in various colours, 21.5 × 298 cm.
Inv. no. c/85/3 / Donated by MKiS in 1951.
Made of four strips; along the entire length, an inscription, incomplete
since the beginning of the wrapper is missing:

...ה נולד ב״מ״ז״ט יום ד׳ זיון אייר תרכא לפק
השם ברוך הו יגדלהו בתורה ולחופה ולמעשים טובים אמן סלה

"... born u[nder a] l[ucky] s[tar] Tuesday 7 Iyyar [5]621 [=1861].
May God be blessed who will make him grow for Torah, for huppah and
for ma'asim tovim. Amen. Selah".
Under this inscription, a band of branches with red berries.
On the third strip, an unrolled Torah scroll with the following inscription:

וזאת התורה אשר שם משה לפני בני ישראל
על פי יי ביד משה
עץ חיים היא למחזיקים בה

"And this is the law which Moses set before the children of Israel on the order of the Omnipotent by Moses. She is a tree of life to them that lay hold upon her..."* (Deut. iv, 44; Prov. iii, 18).
Further on, round the blossom symbolizing huppah, the inscription:

קול ששון וקול שמחה קול חתן וקול כלה

"The voice of mirth, and the voice of gladness, the voice of the bridegroom, and the voice of the bride." (Jer. vii, 34, xvi, 9, xxv, 10, part of the final marriage benediction).

* Initial part of the prayer, composed of excerpts from the Old Testament, said during the risting of the Torah.

27. Torah mantle, Germany?, 1896
Silk, écru ribbed silk, dark red velvet; embroidery on cardboard background and cotton-thread foundation, worked in gilded and silvered metal thread, and gilded metal braiding; inscriptions in silk thread, 45 × 73 cm.
Inv. no. C-7 / Donated by the Municipal Museum in Toruń in 1949.
Dedicatory inscription in Yiddish along the lower hem:

געווידמעט פאן א. קירשטיין
אונד פריא פוילא געב. פאביאן
ת ר נ ו

"Gift of A. Kirshtein and Mme Paula née Fabian".
"[5]656" (=1896).

28. Torah mantle, Greece, second half of the 19th cent.
Dark blue velvet, embroidered in gilded metal and silk thread and gilded metal sequins on cardboard background, 90 × 100 cm.
Inv. no. C-82/1 / Donated by MKiS in 1951. /
Dedicatory inscription: הקדש / דילסידור מרדכי / הלוי הי״ו
היום א תמוז התרפז

"Blessed. From Dilsidor Mordechai Halevi [May] G[od] p[rotect him] and [preserve him] on the 1st day of Tammuz [5]687 [=1927]".
Rabbinical authorities allowed fabrics taken from lay clothes to be used for making liturgical vestments, and this mantle is an example of this.

29. Torah mantle, Greece, second half of the 19th cent.
Dark red velvet, embroidered in gilded metal thread on cardboard background, 98 × 88 cm.
Inv. no. C-82/2 / Donated by MKiS in 1951.

30. Torah mantle, Greece, 1896
Dark red velvet embroidered in gilded metal thread, the crown on green and pink velvet background worked in sequins and colour glass beads, cotton fringe in metal thread, 90 × 95 cm.
Inv. no. C-82/3 / Donated by MKiS in 1951.
Dedicatory inscription: קדש ל״ה / זאת נדבה אשר/ הפרישו מתרומת
כספם היקר הר׳ / יוסף משה חביר׳ הי״ו
ובנו היקר / מרדכי הי״ו לכבוד / אביו ישלם
ה׳ פעלם

"Dedicated to G[od]. This is a gift provided with a money contribution by dear Mr Josef Moshe Chabir [May] G[od] p[rotect] and [preserve him] and his son dear Mordechai [May] G[od] p[rotect] and [preserve him] to honour his father Ishlam Pelm".
At the sides the letters: כ ת "C[rown of the] T[orah]"
In the lower part, the date: שנת (=1896). 5656 /

31. Torah mantle, Salonika, 1893
Purple, green and amaranth velvet embroidered in gilded metal thread worked in flat and raised stitches, 82 × 87 cm.
Inv. no. C-71 / Acquired from the former concentration camp of Auschwitz-Birkenau in 1948.
On both sides of the crown, the letters: כ ת
"The Crown of the Torah".
Dedicatory inscription in a wreath:
קדש ל״ה / מה מנוה החחש כתר / חיים ש עמר נ״ע
נדב מחיים / לק״ק סיסיליה היעא
שהתהרנג תנצבה

"Dedicated to God. From the deceased .... v[enerable] r[abbi] Haim .... [of] b[lessed] m[emory] offering of life for the sacred community of Sisilija* May G[od] [have] m[ercy] o[n us] a[men]".
"Y[ear] [5]653 [=1893]".

* In Salonika there were two synagogues bearing the name of Sisilija — the Old and the New Sisilija — which belonged to immigrants from Sicily. This mantle comes from one of them.

32. Torah Ark curtain, Prussia Silesia, 1774
Green and raspberry velvet embroidered in silvered metal thread, cotton and silk on cardboard and cotton background in flat and raised stitches, 195 × 144 cm.
Inv. no. C-44 / In the ŻIH Museum since 1948.
In the centre, on a rectangular piece of raspberry velvet, a scene of the sacrifice of Isaac with the following inscriptions above its individual elements:

ויקרא אליו מלאך ה — "And the angel of the LORD called unto him..." (Gen. xxii, 11)
עץ חיים — "The tree of life"
יצחק עקדת — "Sacrifice of Isaac"
ויבן שם מזבח — "[Abraham] built an altar there..." (Gen. xxii, 9)
איל בקרניו — "[Abraham lifted up his eyes, and looked, and beheld behind him] a ram [caught in a thicket by his] horns..." (Gen. xxii, 13)

At the top, a crown supported by two lions, with an inscription at its sides:
תורה כתר "The Crown of the Torah"
and below the crown: שויתי / * יהוה / לנגדי תמיד
"I have set the LORD* always before me" (Ps. xvi 8)
In the lower part, surrounded by plant and geometrical ornaments, a scene of circumcision with the following inscription by its sides:
וימל אברהם / את יצחק "Abraham circumcised [his son] Isaac" (Gen. xxi, 4)
Above and below this scene, the following inscriptions:
לפרט ואתנה בריתי ביני וביניך /וארבה אותך במאד מאד
הנדב והיקדש זאת ביום הבכורם בהקריב מנחה חדשה לה
מקרא קדש יהי / לכם יחיאל ברוך חסרו

"And I will make my covenant between me and thee, and will multiply thee exceedingly" (Gen. xvii, 2).
Bequeathed and blessed on Yom ha-Bikkurim** with a new offering to the Lord. "Ye shall have a holy convocation" (Lev. xxiii, 7).
Jehiel in his exceeding benevolence.
The second and fourth words in the first line form the date: [5]534 = 1774.

* According to the original text, the word "Jahve" (יהוה) should appear here. An abbreviation was used on the parokhet.
** Yom ha Bikkurim, or the Day of the First Fruits also called Shavuot, the Feast of Weeks, celebrated seven weeks after the Pesach.

The figural scenes indicate that this parokhet was offered to the synagogue to honour the birth of the first son whose name was probably "Jehiel", on the occasion of his circumcision (Heb. brit milah) and redemption

(Heb. *pidyon ha-ben*). The vessels and other objects used during these ceremonies were frequently adorned with scenes of Abraham's offering. For this reason it was not by chance that the parokhet was offered on Shavuot, the Day of the First Fruits, when in accordance with the biblical prescription that all the first born should be offered to God (Ex. xiii, 2, xxxiv, 19–20, 26; Lew. xxvii, 26; Num. iii, 2, 40–51, xviii, 13, 15–16; Deut. xv, 19) the first crops of grain and fruit were brought to the Temple.

33. Torah Ark curtain with valance, Prussia–Silesia, 1783
Green and light-brown velvet, embroidered in silvered metal thread, cotton and silk on cardboard background in flat and raised stitches, appliqué work, 120 × 162 and 38 × 135 cm.
Inv. no. C-270 / Purchased in 1977.
Inscription above the crown:

כתר תורה   "The Crown of the Torah"

Dedicatory inscription at the sides:

את נדב האלוף / הרר קאפל בן
הרר חיים זל / מטוארגי
ואשתו הצנועה / מרת חיי בת
מ˜ אברהם זצל / מפרוסקא

"Gift of Master Kopel son of Chaim [of] b[lessed] m[emory] of Tworóg and his wife virtuous Chaia daughter of M[aster] Abraham [of] b[lessed] m[emory] of Prószków."

Inscription in the lower part, between the plinths:

בשנת
לא הביט און ביעקב
ולא ראה עמל בישראל

"In the year
He hath not beheld iniquity in Jacob, neither hath he seen perverseness in Israel." (Num. xxiii, 21)

The last word of the quotation indicates the year [5]543 (=1783)
Tworóg and Prószków are situated in Lower Silesia.

34. Torah Ark curtain, Poland?, late 17th cent.
Red velvet, embroidered in silvered and gilded metal thread on cotton and cardboard background, with braiding and appliqué work, 260 × 187 cm.
Inv. no. C-266 / Purchased in 1975.

Inscription to the right:

נפשנו תקריב נוכח
פני יודע יצרנו טוב
לבבנו
לפרט חקת התרה

May our soul be dedicated
to the Lord of our will
and our sincere hearts
acc. to the date, The Ordinance
of the Law*
(Num. xix, 2) [5]508 (=1748)

Inscription to the left:

ולמכסה ארון של חן
תבה והתורה
עדיים
לשבת קודש רימונו

And in order to cover
the beautiful box of the
Ark and the Torah
the gems of the holy Sabbath
...

* The name and the first words of the sixth parashah from the Book of Numbers.

35. Torah Ark curtain, Germany, 1872
Cream-coloured silk damask, unbleached cotton, green ribbed silk, embroidered in silvered metal thread on cardboard background, silvered metal sequins, appliqué-work crown, 317 × 140 cm.
Inv. no. C-45 / Donated by the Municipal Museum in Toruń in 1949.
Inscription at the sides of the crown: "The Crown of the Torah"
Inscription in the wreath:

תקעו בחדש שופר / בכסה ליום חגנו
כי חק לישראל הוא / משפט לאלהי יעקב
כי ביום הזה יכפר עליכם
לטהר אתכם מכל חטאתיהם / לפני יהוה / תטהרו

"At full moon blow the shofars during the ceremony of the day of our feast. Since this is the decree for Israel, the law from Jacob's God." (excerpt from the additional prayer *Musaf* for Rosh ha-Shana, Ps. LXXXI,4).
"For on this day we forgive you in order to cleanse you of all sins, before the Omnipotent you will be cleansed." (excerpt from the additional prayer *Musaf* for Yom Kippur).
Inscription in the centre of the circle entwined in acanthus branches:

נדבת לב / לכבוד התורה והעבודה
מאת שמעון בן ר משה יחיאל / קירכהיים
מפ˜פ על המיין / וזוגתו ערנעזטינא בת החבר
ר נתן לייזער מטהארן / ביום התונתם לג בעומר
תרלב לפ˜ק

"Offering of the heart / To the glory of the Torah and religion from Simon son of r[abbi] Moshe Jehiel Kirkheim of Fr[ankfurt] on the Main and his spouse Ernestine daughter of Nathan Leizer of Toruń. On the day of their wedding in Lag Ba-Omer. [5]632 [=1872]."
The parokhet came probably from the synagogue at Szczytna street in Toruń.
As the inscription and colour indicate, it was meant to be used on Yom Kippur and Rosh ha-Shana, since the white colour was obligatory on those feast days.

36. Torah Ark curtain, Turkey, late 19th cent.
Silk damask of cream colour, embroidered in silvered and gilded metal thread on cotton and cardboard background, 88 × 90 cm.
Inv. no. C-86/2 / Acquired from the Majdanek Concentration Camp.

37. Cover for the cantor's desk, Turkey, late 19th cent.
Silk damask of cream colour, embroidered in silvered and gilded metal thread on cotton and cardboard background, 44 × 42 cm.
Inv. no. C-86/1 / Acquired from the Majdanek Concentration Camp.
Both the curtain and tablecloth described above form a set. They originated in the same workshop and were made of the same kind of material by means of the same techniques and using identical ornamental motifs. The symbols applied – birds (peacocks and swallows), flowers, pomegranates and the sign of the ruler – are all in keeping with the conventions of Jewish religious fabrics. Only the representation of a mosque (or perhaps of Jerusalem where, instead of the temple, views of mosques with their minarets are shown) suggests that originally it may have been a secular fabric later used for liturgical purposes. We cannot rule out the possibility that they were made in Poland – at Brody which boasted a manufactory producing fabrics with eastern patterns. This version is contradicted only by the monogram: the dates indicate that this is the monogram of Sultan Abdul-Hamid II who ruled in the years 1876–1909.

38. Pair of candlesticks, Vienna, 1840, Monogrammist "AV"
Silver, punched, 30.5 × 14.4 and 29.5 × 14.4 cm.
Signed: (1) Austrian state mark dating from 1806–66: letter "A" (for Vienna), standard "13", year "1840"; (2) goldsmith's mark: letters "AV" ("A" without horizontal bar) in a rectangle.
Inv. no. C-277/a,b / Gift of Janina Kuczyńska in 1982.

39. Pair of candlesticks, Vienna, late 19th cent., Monogrammist "H.S."
Silver, punched, 45 × 16 × 16 cm.
Signed: (1) Austrian-Hungarian state mark dating from 1872–1922: right female profile in a cinquefoil, standard "3", letter "A" (for Vienna); (2) goldsmith's mark: initials "H.S." in a rectangle.
Inv. no. C-170/a,b / Purchased in 1961.

40. Candlestick, Warsaw, after 1852, Jan Pogorzelski, Warsaw goldsmith active before 1851, his company operated until ca. 1910

Silver, punched and cast, 38,5 × 13,8 × 13,8 cm.
Signed: (1) goldsmith's name "POGORZELSKI" in a rectangle; (2) work-shop device: elk's head in an oval; (3) standard "84" in an oval and letter "S" horizontally to the right.
Inv. no. C-186 / Donated by CKHwŁ 1947.

41. Candlestick, Warsaw, Konstanty Wolski's factory of bronze, silver and gold ware specializing in the production of chandeliers, candelabra and candleholders, 20th cent.*
Metal punched and silvered, 25,5 × 12 × 12 cm.
Signed: (1) in a rectangle "FABR.WOLS."; (2) "AA/165".
Inv. no. C-172 / Donated by CKHwŁ in 1947.

* It may have also been produced by Wolski F. and Co. of silver-plated and bronze ware.

42. Candlestick, Warsaw, Fraget, 20th cent.
Metal punched and silvered, 30,4 × 12,5 × 12 cm.
Signed: (1) maker's device: "FRAGET/W/WARSZAWIE" in an oval, "GALW." in a rectangle, clover? leaf in a circle, letter "N" (?) in an oval; (2) band of vertical notches in an oval, letters "SEC" in a rectangle, no. "2103".
Inv. no. C-187 / Donated by CKHwŁ in 1947.

43. Pair of candlesticks, Silesia? 19th cent.
Silver, punched, 38 × 15.5 × 15.5 cm.
Signed: standard "12" in a square.
Inv. no C-253/a,b / Donated by CKŻwP branch in Katowice in 1949.
Owner's name: LOUISE / HAASE
These candlesticks probably come from the synagogue in Rybnik.

44. Cup, Moscow, 1878
Silver, punched and engraved, 6.5 × 5.7 × 3.5 cm.
Signed: (1) Russian state mark: assay officer's initials "IK" in cyrillic, year "1878", standard "84", coat of arms showing St. George on horseback killing the dragon (for Moscow); (2) goldsmith's initials "L" in cyrillic with the second letter undecipherable.
Inv. no. C-325 / Gift of Bolesław Szenicer in 1986.

45. Goblet, Vienna, 1846
Silver, punched, repoussé and engraved, 10.5 × 5 × 5 cm.
Signed: (1) Austrian state mark dating from 1806–66: letter "A" (for Vienna), standard "13", year "1846".
Inv. no. C-264 / Gift of Franciszek Kalinowski in 1974.

46. Goblet, Cracow, 1922–9, Monogrammist "JO"
Silver, punched, engraved, 11.2 × 5.7 × 5.2 cm.
Signed: (1) Polish state hall-mark dating from 1922–1933: standard "3", letter "K" (for Kraków – Cracow), (2) goldsmith's mark – initials "JO" in a circle.
Inv. no. C-324 / Donated by the State Treasury in 1988.

47. Goblet, Kiev, 1908–17, Monogrammist "G.R."
Silver, punched, engraved and gilded, 6.4 × 3.5 × 3.5 cm.
Signed: (1) Russian state mark dating from 1908–17: Greek letter v (for Kiev), right profile of a woman's head in a kokoshnik, standard "84"; (2) goldsmith's mark: cyrillic monogram "G.R." in a square.
Inv. no. C-200 / Unknown origin.

48. Cup, Moscow, 1888, Monogrammist "PD"
Silver, punched, engraved and gilded, 5 × 4.5 × 2.5 cm.
Signed: (1) Russian state mark: assay officer's initials "V.S." in cyrillic (Viktor Savinkov 1855–88), year "1888", standard "84", coat of arms

showing St. George on horseback (for Moscow); (2) goldsmith's mark: initials "PD" in cyrillic in a square.
Inv. no. C-326 / Donated by the State Treasury in 1988.

49. Goblet, Poland?, 1890
Silver, punched and engraved, 17.5 × 8.5 cm.
Inv. no. C-196 / Donated by Joint in 1950.
Dedicatory inscription:
Gewidmet (von) I. Pinczower (1890 / Donated by I. Pinczower 1890).

50. Goblet, Cracow, 1922–39, Monogrammist "IH"
Silver, punched, engraved and gilded, 12 × 5.4 × 4.8 cm.
Signed: (1) Polish state hall-mark dating from 1922–39: standard "3", letter "K" (for Cracow or Kraków); (2) goldsmith's mark: initials "IH" in an oval.
Inv. no. C-292 / Donated by the Voivodship Monument Conservator in Radom in 1983.
Dedicatory inscription: מ״ד / מאדמו״ר שליט״א / מקאושעניץ
P[reacher of] W[isdom] O[ur] L[ord] T[eacher] M[aster] [May He] L[ive] L[ong and] H[appily] A[men] Kozienice".
Kozienice became a centre of Hasidism in the late 18th century, with the arrival of the famous zaddik, Israel Ben Shabbetai Hapstein (1733–1814), called the Maggid of Kozienice, the founder of a hasidic dynasty. This cup may have been offered to one of his successors, either zaddik Asher Elimelech (d. 1936) or zaddik Aaron Jehiel (d. 1942).

51. Goblet, Moscow, 1875, Monogrammist "IL"
Silver, chased, engraved and gilded, 10 × 5.4 × 6.2 cm.
Signed: (1) Russian state mark; assay officer's initials "L.S." in cyrillic, year "1875", standard "84", coat of arms showing St. George killing the dragon (for Moscow); (2) goldsmith's mark: initials "IL" in cyrillic in a rectangle.
Inv. no. C-194 / Unknown origin.
Dedicatory inscription: לאדמו״ר רשכבה״ג הגאון ר׳ יצחק אלחנן ספעקטאר / מנחה שלוחה למזכרת עולם / מאת יוסף בן שאול עזרא מקאוקאז חאסאף יורט / טערסקי אבלאסט שנת תרמח קאוונא
"For our Lord, Teacher, Master of the whole diaspora the Gaon rabbi Isaac Elhanan Spektor a gift given in eternal memory from Josef son of Saul Ezra of the Caucassus Chasaf Yurt oblast Tersk [5] 648 (=1888) Kovno".
Isaac Elhanan Spektor (1817–96), a Lithuanian rabbi, lived and died in Kovno. One of the recognized rabbinical authorities in the world, founder of a yeshivah, author of several commentaries to *Shulhan Arukh* and responsa.

52. Synagogal goblet, Berlin, 1900
Silver, punched and engraved, 22.5 × 11.5 × 9 cm.
Signed: (1) Prussian state mark dating from 1888: standard "800", a crescent and crown; (2) workshop device: letter "A", no. "20743", cup.
Inv. no. C-193 / Donated by the Municipal Museum in Toruń in 1949.
Dedicatory inscription:
Der Synagoge Culmsee gewidmet von Ludwig Gertrud Latte Berlin, zum 1 Tischri 5660 (= 1900) (Offered to the synagogue in Chełmża by Ludwig Gertrud Latté in Berlin, on the last day of Tishri 5660 (=1900)).
Inscription in the centre: זכור / את יום השבת / לקדשו
"Remember the sabbath day, to keep it holy" (Ex. xx, 8)

Culmsee, or Chełmża, in the Chełmno area which became part of the Kingdom of Prussia after the first partition of Poland in 1772.

53. Cup, Moscow, 1908–17, Vasili Semenov's factory established in 1852
Silver, punched and engraved, 7 × 5 × 4 cm.
Signed: (1) Russian state mark dating fron 1908–17: Greek letter Δ (for

Moscow), right profile of a woman's head in a kokoshnik, standard "84";
(2) maker's device: cyrillic letters "VS" in a square.
Inv. no. C-282 / Gift of Władysław Sobczyński in 1983.

54. Goblet, Kiev, 1908–17, Monogrammist "G.R."
Silver, punched, engraved and gilded, 9 × 3 × 3.3 cm.
Signed: (1) Russian state mark dating from 1908–17: Greek letter *v* (for Kiev), right profile of a woman's head in a kokoshnik, standard "84"; (2) goldsmith's mark: cyrillic monogram "G.R."; (3) Polish state mark dating from 1922–39: standard "2", left profile of a female head, letter "W" (for Warsaw); (4) Polish pawn-shop mark dating from after 1922.
Inv. no. C-327 / Donated by the State Treasury in 1988.

55. Cup, Russia, 1896 1908
Silver, punched, engraved and gilded, 6.4 × 5.5 × 3.5 cm.
Signed: (1) Russian state mark dating from 1896–1908: in an oval, left profile of a woman's head in a kokoshnik, standard "84", assay officer's initials "AA"; (2) goldsmith's mark: initials "P.PG./OR" in cyrillic in a square with cut corners.
Inv. no. C-202 / Unearthed; gift, 1949.

56. Cup, Poland, first half of the 19th cent.
Silver, punched and engraved, 6.5 × 6 × 4.3 cm.
Signed: (1) standard "12" in a square; (2) in a rectangle, goldsmith's name in italics, with only the last letters "...kiel" decipherable.
Inv. no. C-287 / Gift of Mieczysław Eibel in 1983.

57. Spice box, Austria, early 19th cent.
Silver, cast, filigree, engraved, with traces of gilding, 18 × 4.6 × 4.6 cm.
Inv. no. C-102 / Donated by Joint in 1950.

58. Spice box, Austria, before 1809
Silver, filigree, punched, with traces of gilding, 22.5 × 4.6 cm.
Signed: 11 marks, in these decipherable: (1) Austrian hall-mark dating from 1809 10 releasing larger objects from a fee towards the State Treasury; (2) initials "SŁ."?
Inv. no. C-107 / Donated by Joint in 1950.

59. Spice box, Brno, early 19th cent.
Silver, cast, filigree, engraved, 18 × 5.9 cm.
Signed: (1) Austrian contribution mark dating from 1806 09: crescent and letter "F" (for Brno); (2) Austrian hall-mark for small objects in silver, which released them from a fee towards the State Treasury, dating from 1809 10.
Inv. no. C-122 / Donated by Joint in 1950.

60. Spice box, Moscow, 1870's
Silver, filigree, punched, 10 × 4 cm.
Signed: (1) Russian state mark: assay officer's initials "V.S." in cyrillic (Victor Savinkov, 1855–88), year "186...", undecipherable workshop device.
Inv. no. C-100 / Donated by Joint in 1950.

61. Spice box, Austria, first half of the 19th cent.
Silver, filigree, punched, cast, with traces of gilding, 16.7 × 4.5 cm.
Inv. no. C-105 / Donated by Joint in 1950.

62. Spice box, Lvov, 1852
Silver, filigree, punched, 24.3 × 5.7 × 5.7 cm.
Signed: (1) Austrian state mark dating from 1806 66: letter "D" (for

Lvov), year "1852", standard "13"; (2) Polish state mark dating from 1922–39: standard "3", letter "L" (for Lvov).
Inv. no. C-133 / Donated by Joint in 1950.

63. Spice box, Germany?, 19th cent.
Silver, filigree, punched and engraved, 27 × 6.3 cm.
Inv. no. C-115 / Donated by Joint in 1950.

64. Spice box, Warsaw, 1896–1908, M. Charlap
Silver, punched, cast, engraved and gilded, 24 × 5.9 cm.
Signed: (1) hall-mark of the Warsaw assay office from 1896–1908: standard "84", left profile of a woman's head in a kokoshnik hat, assay officer's initials "AP"; (2) goldsmith's mark: name "M". "CHARŁAP" in cyrillic in a rectangle.
Inv. no. C-106 / Donated by CKHwŁ in 1947.

65. Spice box, Poland, early 19th cent.
Silver, punched, cast and engraved, 21.5 × 4.5 × 4.5 cm.
Inv. no. C-114 / Donated by Joint in 1950.

66. Spice box, first half of the 19th cent.
Silver, filigree, repoussé with traces of gilding, 17.5 × 7.4 cm.
Signed: (1) standard "12" in a square; (2) undecipherable mark.
Inv. no. C-91 / Donated by Joint in 1950.

67. Spice box, Warsaw, 1828 50, Karol Filip Malcz (1797 1867), Warsaw goldsmith active from 1828
Silver, punched, cast and engraved, with traces of gilding, 24.4 × 7 cm.
Signed: (1) goldsmith's mark: obliterated name "Malcz" in italics, in a rectangle with rounded corners; (2) device of the workshop: an anchor in an oval; (3) standard "12" in a square with cut corners.
Inv. no. C-319 / Purchased in 1987.

68. Spice box, Warsaw, 1896 1910, Antoni Riedel, Warsaw goldsmith active in 1878–1910
Silver, punched, cast and engraved, with traces of gilding, 15.5 × 8.5 cm.
Signed: (1) goldsmith's mark: name "A. RIEDEL" in a rectangle; (2) workshop device: stirrup; (3) hall-mark of the Warsaw assay office dating from 1896 1908: standard "84", left profile of a woman's head in a kokoshnik, assay officer's initials "AP".
Inv. no. C-96 / Donated by Joint in 1950.

69. Etrog container, Moscow, 1844, Pavel Sazikov, campany established in 1793 by Pavel Fedorovich Sazikov, from 1842 on with a branch in St. Petersburg
Silver, punched, cast, gilded and oxidized, 12 × 27 cm.
Signed: (1) Russian state mark: assay officer's initials "A.K.", year "1844", standard "84", coat of arms of Moscow showing St. George on horseback killing the dragon; (2) goldsmith's initials "P.S." and surname "SAZI-KOV" in cyrillic.
Inv. no. C-322 / Donated by the State Treasury in 1988.

70. Hanukkah lamp, Poland, 19th/20th cent.
Brass, cast, 16.2 × 21.3 cm.
Inv. no. C-177 / Donated by CKHwŁ in 1947.
Inscription: להדליק נר חנוכה
"Lighting the Hanukkah lamp", from the benediction uttered before the lighting of the Hanukkah lamp.

71. Hanukkah lamp, Silesia?, first half of the 19th cent.
Brass, cast, 103 × 122 cm.

Signed: (1) maker's mark "GERST" in a rectangle, (2) device of the workshop: head of stag or elk in a left profile.
In. no. C-339 / Donated by MKiS in 1951.

72. Hanukkah lamp, Eastern Europe, early 19th cent.
Silver, filigree, engraved, cast, granulated filigree ornamented with applied rhombuses, 29 × 31.7 × 9.1 cm.
Inv. no. C-155 / Donated by Joint in 1950.

73. Hanukkah lamp, Warsaw, 1871, Abraham Reiner, Warsaw goldsmith active between the 1840's and 1870's
Silver, repoussé, cast, 20 × 19.5 × 6 cm.
Signed: (1) goldsmith's mark: "Reiner" in italics in a rectangle; (2) workshop device: a stag running left in an oval; (3) Warsaw hallmark dating from 1851–96: assay officer's initials "O.C.", year "1871", standard "84", and a two-headed eagle.
Inv. no. C-189 / Donated by CKHwŁ in 1947.

74. Hanukkah lamp, Warsaw, second half of the 19th cent., Fraget
Metal, punched, cast and silvered, 29.5 × 24.5 cm.
Signed: maker's device: a crowned two-headed eagle with the armorial shield of the Kingdom of Poland on its breast; in an oval, inscription "FRAGET/N/PLAQUE", a clover? leaf, no. "1946".
Inv. no. C-271 / Purchased in 1978.

75. Hanukkah lamp, Warsaw, 19th cent. (after 1893) or 20th cent., Norblin, a factory of silver-plated ware established in 1809 by W. K. Norblin. Following mergers with, successively, A. T. Werner, Buch Bros. and T. Temler and Co., it was active till 1939 under the name of Norblin, Buch Bros. and T. Werner Co. of metal factories
Metal, punched, cast, silvered, with traces of gilding, 31.5 × 34 × 7.5 cm.
Signed: (1) device of the company: a swan in a circle, with a six-pointed star above; in an oval inscription "NORBLIN et C° WARSZAWA/GALW", no. "234"; (2) unidentified device.
Inv. no. C-165 / Donated by CKHwŁ in 1947.

76. Hanukkah lamp, Eastern Europe, 18th/19th cent.
Brass, cast, 27 × 23.5 cm.
Inv. no. C-299 / Gift, 1984.

77. Hanukkah lamp, Poland, 19th/20th cent.
Brass, cast, 16.5 × 14.2 cm.
Inv. no. C-167 / Donated by CKHwŁ in 1947.

78. Hanukkah lamp, Poland?, 19th cent.
Brass, cast, 37 × 33 × 12 cm.
Inv. no. C-179 / Donated by CKHwŁ in 1947.

79. Hanukkah lamp, Warsaw, second half of the 19th cent., Fraget, a firm active in 1824–1939, specializing in silver-plated wares and also silverware.
Metal, punched, cast, silvered and gilded, 23.3 × 22.5 cm.
Signed: (1) device of the firm: a crowned two-headed eagle with the armorial shield of the Kingdom of Poland on its breast; in an oval, inscription "FRAGET/N/PLAQUE", a clover? leaf in an oval, no. "1945".
Inv. no. C-164 / Purchased in 1948.

80. Scroll of Esther, Złotów? Złoczów?, first half of the 19th cent.
Parchment illuminated in ink and tempera, hand-written, 28.3 × 295 cm.
Signed: סליק המגילה אני הצייר נתן בן הרר יוסף
סופר סתם בקק זלאטווי
"The end of the megillat. I, Natan, son of Józef, scribe of holy books,

tefillins and mezuzoth from the sacred community of Złotów?, am the artist".
Inv. no. C-254 / Donated by MKiS.
Illustrations in this Megillat recall polychromes in Polish synagogues.

81. Esther Scroll case, Jerusalem, 1906–29, Bezalel
Etched silver, filigree, punched and oxidized, set with chrysoprases, 22.5 × 3.5 cm.
Inv. no. C-236 / Donated by Joint in 1950.
Inscription below the central medallion: ותגע בראש השרביט
"[So Esther drew near,] and touched the top of the sceptre" (Esth. v. 2).
Inscription amidst ornaments round the medallion:
מגלת אסתר (Megillat Esther).

82. Esther Scroll case, Persia?, 19th/20th cent.
Metal, punched, engraved and silvered, 21 × 4 cm.
Inv. no. C-234 / Donated by Joint in 1950.

83. Scroll of Esther, Austria?, 18th/19th cent.
Illuminated parchment, hand-written, ink and tempera, 32.5 × 277 cm.
Inv. no. C-254 / Donated by MKiS in 1951.

84. Scroll of Esther, Bohemia, mid-18th cent.
Illuminated parchment, hand-written, sepia, 19 × 159.5 cm.
Inv. no. C-254 / Donated by MKiS in 1951.

85. Matzah bag, Łódź?, 1912
White ribbed silk and linen, embroidered in shaded patterns worked in cotton, silk and metal threads, partly on cotton foundation; hemmed with a double line of tulle lace and braiding, diameter 50 cm.
Inv. no. C-30 / Found in the Łódź ghetto in 1948.
Made in the form of an oval with three compartments, each with a triangular flap carrying the following inscriptions:
"Israel" ישראל   "Levite" לוי   "Priest" כהן
On its top, in the upper part, a crown embellished with glass beads, with, at its sides, the inscription: סדר של פסח
"Seder feast", and letters: מ / א
Under the crown, a lamb on a grid. In the centre, a semi-circular flower wreath with the following inscription below:
זכר ליציאת מצרים תרעב   "In memory of the departure from Egypt [5]672 [=1912]
לשנה הבאה בירושלים   Next year in Jerusalem".

86. Seder plate, Germany?, first half of the 19th cent.
Hand-painted faience, diameter 24.4 cm.
Signed: (1) a circle divided radially into eight fields; (2) figure "1".
Inv. no. C-220 / Purchased in 1948.
The centre of the plate yellow, covered in rich geometrical plant ornaments (including stylized acanthus blossoms and leaves).
The ornaments surround six circles carrying the names of symbolic Seder dishes:

(baytsa) ביצה	(maror) מרור	(zeroa) זרוע
(karpas) כרפס	(chazeret) חזרת	(charoset) חרוסת

In the upper part of the plate, the Paschal lamb. The blue rim decorated with sixteen cartouches with the names indicating the order of Seder observances:

(karpas) כרפס	(rechac) ורחץ	(kadesh) קדש
(rachca) רחצה	(magid) מגיד	(yachac) יחץ
(maror) מרור	(matzah) מצה	(motzi) מוציא

23

(arukh) עורך	(shulhan) שלחן	(korech) כורך
(hallel) הלל	(barech) ברך	(cafun) צפון
		(nirca)* נרצה

The seventeenth, largest cartouche bears at the top the inscription:
(Seder / plate) סדר / הקערה

* The Seder meal is composed of fourteen observances. On this particular plate, for reasons of composition, the names of two of them – motzi matzah and shulhan arukh – are each placed on two separate cartouches.

87. Plate, Jerusalem, 1906–29, Bezalel
Engraved brass, inlaid with silver and copper (Damascene workmanship), diameter 29.7 cm.
Signed: בצלאל (Bezalel) inlaid in copper.
Inv. no. C-206 / Purchased in 1948.
Inscription in the centre: בצלאל (Bezalel)
Inscription in six oval fields: אם אשכחך ירושלם תשכח ימיני תדבק לשוני לחכי
אם לא אזכרכי אסל.

> If I forget thee, O Jerusalem,
> let my right hand forget her cunning.
> If I do not remember thee,
> let my tongue cleave to the roof of my mouth.
>   (Ps. cxxxvii, 5–6)

This quotation shows that the plate may have been used as a mizrach (east in Hebrew), or an ornamental picture hung on the wall during the Pesach. Jews living in the Diaspora hoped to eventually return to the city of Jerusalem. Hence the custom of decorating the eastern wall of their homes and synagogues with mizraches, or painted, printed or embroidered tablets to indicate the symbolic direction of the holy city. To the dispersed Jews the words of the psalm and the whole ceremony of the Pesach have also another meaning: to them the Seder meal is both a commemoration of historic events and an expression of hope that God one day will show His kindness and restore the Promised Land to the chosen people. This belief in a return to Jerusalem recurs in the Pesach Haggadah, or the tale of the miraculous exodus from Egypt, which the master of the house recites during the Seder, ending with the words: "Next year in Jerusalem".

88. Vessel for washing hands, Jerusalem, 1906–29, Bezalel
Repoussé bronze, inlaid with silver and copper (Damascene workmanship), 11 × 11.3 × 14.4 cm.
Signed: inscription בצלאל (Bezalel) inlaid in copper.
Inv. no. C-208 / Purchased in 1948.
Inscriptions:
בצלאל (Bezalel) התרענן (refreshed himself)
ירושלם (Jerusalem)
Bezalel, an arts and crafts school, established in Jerusalem in 1906 by Boris Schatz (1867–1932), court sculptor to King Ferdinand I of Bulgaria. The school operated until 1929 and was revived in 1935 as the New Bezalel, under Józef Budko. Its name is associated with the biblical craftsman Bezaleel who supervised the construction of the first Sanctuary (Ex. xxxv, 30–33).

89. Vessels for washing hands, Warsaw, 20th cent.
Silver-plated, beaker 9 × 5.5 cm. bowl 9 × 6 cm.
Signed: maker's device in an oval: GALW. / W / PRAGE
The set is composed of a bowl and a beaker.
Inv. no. C-198 and C-305 / Donated by CKŻwŁ in 1947.
Inscription: על מים אחרונים
(Al Maim Achatonim – the last waters)

90. Canopy, Poland?, 19th cent.
Green velvet, cream-coloured silk embroidered in flower motifs, 182 × 180 cm.
Inv. no. C-47 / Purchased in 1948.
This canopy lacks the characteristic symbols and inscriptions typical of nuptial canopies. Therefore it may have been used both during wedding ceremonies and on other occasions, for example in processions involving the transfer of newly offered Torah scrolls to the synagogue.

91. Wedding canopy, Germany?, 1891
Green velvet, brocade, embroidered in silvered metal thread and sequins, 155 × 155 cm.
Inv. no. C-46 / Donated by the Municipal Museum in Toruń in 1949.
Inscription: קול ששון וקול שמחה קול חתן וקול כלה
"The voice of mirth, and the voice of gladness, the voice of the bridegroom, and the voice of the bride" (Jer. vii, 34, xvi, 9, xxv, 10, the final blessing during the marriage ceremony).
In the centre, the date: תרנא "[5]651" (=1891)

92. Atarah, Eastern Europe, 19th cent.
Non-woven openwork on cotton background, with silver braiding, 8 × 68 cm.
Inv. no. C-237 / Donated by Joint in 1950.

93. Atarah, Eastern Europe, 19th cent.
Made of silver spangles in the form of crowns and with a stamped motif of a crown, joined together with links into six rows of 59 elements each; the whole attached to canvas lining, 9 × 95 cm.
Inv. no. C-79 / Donated by MKiS in 1951.

94. Atarah, Eastern Europe, 19th cent.
Non-woven openwork on cotton background, with silver and gilded braiding, 10.5 × 81.5 cm.
Inv. no. C-36 / Purchased in 1948.

95. Atarah, Eastern Europe, 19th cent.
Non-woven openwork (*spanyer arbet* in Yiddish) on cotton background, with braiding of silver, gilded, plain and pearl string, 13.5 × 97 cm.
Inv. no. C-241 / Purchased in 1948.

96. Atarah, Eastern Europe, 19th cent.
Non-woven openwork on cotton background, with silver, plain and pearl braiding, 10.5 × 84 cm.
Inv. no. C-35 / Purchased in 1948.

97. Yarmulke, Eastern Europe, 19th cent.
Embroidered in metal thread on cotton background with gilded silver braiding, 14 × 18.5 cm.
Inv. no. C-317 / Purchased in 1986.
It is possible that the custom originated from the rule ordering Jews to wear hats of special shapes in public places. The rule was established to distinguish and discriminate Jews. Thus, hats of various shapes, depending on the local tradition in each country, started to be worn.

98. Walking stick, Poland, 19th cent.
Mahogany, silver, mother of pearl, 90 cm.
Inv. no. C-251 / Purchased in 1948.
The stick comes probably from the court of the rabbi of Turzysk (now in the Ukraine).

HENRYK (HENOCH, ENRICO) GLICENSTEIN
99. Messiah
Bronze, 67.5 cm / Signed: H. Glicenstein
Inv. no. A-1012 / Purchased in 1948.

MAKS HANEMAN (HANNEMAN)
100. The Wailing Wall
Oil on canvas, 86.5 × 65.5 cm / Signed: Maks Haneman מ. חנמן
Inv. no. A-367 / Purchased in 1961.

SZYMON BUCHBINDER
101. Jew in Prayer
Oil on cardboard, 26.2 × 16.8 cm / Signed: Buchbinder (?)
Inv. no. A-102 / Purchased in 1948.

ROBERT STRASSBERG
102. Ecstasy, 1935
Washed ink, 85.8 × 62.3 cm / Signed: Norbert Strassberg Lwów 1935
Inv. no. A-68 / Purchased in 1949.

JÓZEF BUDKO
103. Thou Shalt not, 1929
Wood engraving on tissue paper, 25.7 × 19.6 cm / Signed: Budko 1929
Inv. no. B. 443/39 / Donated by the Ministry of Culture and Art in 1951.

ANTONI (NACHUM) ALSTER
104. Old Jew, 1963
Wood engraving, 27.5 × 44 cm / Signed: AA
Inv. no. A-1211 / Gift of Leokadia Alster in 1977.

105. Jews with Torah, 1965
Linocut, 32.6 × 31.2 cm / Signed: Alster 1965
Inv. no. A-1208 / Gift of Leokadia Alster in 1977.

TADEUSZ POPIEL
106. The Joy of the Torah (Simhath Torah)
Oil on canvas, 90 × 165 cm / Signed: T. Popiel
Deposit no. 9.

UNKNOWN PAINTER
107. Rabbi with Torah
Oil on canvas, 62.8 × 50.2 cm / Signed: Maler Kaufman
Inv. no. A-334 / Purchased in 1949.
Copy of the painting *Rabbi with Torah* by Izydor Kaufman (1853–1921) with the latter's signature forged.

ARTUR MARKOWICZ
108. Prayer
Oil on canvas, 26.3 × 39.8 cm
Inv. no. A-508 / Purchased in 1947.

FRYDERYK (FRYC) KLEINMAN
109. Jews with Torah, 1933
Oil on canvas, 101 × 80 cm / Signed: Fryc Kleinman 933
Inv. no. A-164.

MANE KATZ (EMANUEL KATZ)
110. Rabbi with Torah
Ink and sepia on paper, 35.5 × 25.7 cm / Signed: Mané-Katz.
Inv. no. A-1405 / Gift of Ernestyna Podhorizer-Sandel in 1984.

ZYGMUNT MENKES
111. Jew with Torah
Lithograph, sanguine, 35 × 25.5 cm / Signed: Menkes
Inv. no. B-443/52 / Donated by the Ministry of Culture and Art in 1951.

ARTUR MARKOWICZ
112. Sanctification of the New Moon (Kiddush levanah)
Pastel on cardboard, 57 × 47.5 cm
Inv. no. A-1457 / Gift of Ernestyna Podhorizer-Sandel in 1984.

WŁADYSŁAW LESZCZYŃSKI
113. Jew Praying at Night, 1887
Oil on canvas, 20.2 × 14.1 cm / Signed: W. Leszczyński 1887
Inv. no. A-625 / In the ŻIH Museum since 1959.

ARTUR RENNERT
114. Spice Boxes
Lithograph, 50 × 25.8 cm / Signed: AR
Inv. no. A-1346 / Gift of the artist in 1980.

RACHELA MARCUS-SZALIT
115. Sabbath, 1923
Lithograph, 30.8 × 20.5 cm / Signed: Rahel Szalit-Marcus 1923
Inv. no. B-443/36 / Donated by the Ministry of Culture and Art in 1951.

ADOLF (ABRAHAM) MESSER
116. Reading the Book, 1928
Oil on canvas, 58 × 70 cm / Signed: A. Messer Kraków 1928
Inv. no. A-39.

A. STEIN
117. Reading the Book
Oil on cardboard, 42.3 × 61.2 cm / Signed: A. Stein
Inv. no. A-281 / Gift of Efroim Hofman.
Copy of the painting *Teacher and a Jewish Child Asleep over the Talmud* by Antoni Józef Kamiński (1823–86), at present in the collection of the State Archaeological Museum in Warsaw, inv. no. PMA-J-30/86.

ARTUR MARKOWICZ
118. Talmudists, 1922
Pastel and gouache on cardboard, 19 × 19 cm / Signed: Artur/Markowicz/Kraków/1922
Inv. no. A-1203 / Gift of S. Hutterer of Antwerp in 1977.

MAURYCY GOTTLIEB
119. Head of an Old Man, c. 1875
Oil on canvas, 52.6 × 47.8 cm / Signed: M. Gottlieb
Inv. no. A-37 / Purchased in 1949.

MAURYCY TRĘBACZ
120. Portrait of an Old Man (Ben Akiba)
Oil on canvas, 72.5 × 53 cm / Signed: Maurycy Trębacz/Warszawa/18....
Inv. no. A-24 / Donated by Joint.

ZYGMUNT NADEL
121. Jew in a Fur Hat Holding the Tallith
Oil on canvas, 115 × 80 cm / Signed: Nadel
Inv. no. A-148 / Purchased.

122. Beggar
Oil on canvas, 106 × 74 cm / Signed: Nadel
Inv. no. A-405 / Purchased.

WILHELM WACHTEL
123. Study of a Jewish Boy, 1916
Pastel, 51 × 40.5 cm / Signed: Wilh. Wachtel 1916
Inv. no. A-697 / Purchased in 1947.

MAKSYMILIAN ELJOWICZ
124. Rabbi
Lithograph, 62.8 × 44.1 cm / Signed: Maks Eljowicz
Inv. no. A-135 / Gift, 1947.

ANTONI GRABARZ JARZYMSKI
125. Jewish Furrier, 1937
Oil on canvas, 102 × 82 cm / Signed: Antoni Grabarz 1937
Inv. no. A-4 / Purchased.

SAMUEL HIRSZENBERG
126. Jew with a Walking Stick, 1902
Oil on canvas, 75 × 48.5 cm / Signed: S. Hirszenberg Łódź 1902
Inv. no. A-446 / Purchased.

LEON LEWKOWICZ
127. Head of an Old Man, 1921
Oil on canvas, cardboard, 45.7 × 31.6 cm / Signed: Leon Lewkowicz/21
Inv. no. A-315 / Purchased in 1949.

ARTUR MARKOWICZ
128. Jew at Work
Pastel on cardboard, 39 × 31 cm / Signed: Artur/Markowicz/Kraków
Inv. no. A-479 / In the ŻIH Museum since 1963.

MOJŻESZ (MAURYCY) RYNECKI
129. Jew at Work (In the Carding Shop)
Watercolour on cardboard, 35 × 49 cm / Signed: M. Rynecki
Inv. no. A-1356 / Purchased in 1949.

JOACHIM KAHANE
130. Head of a Jew, 1936
Repoussé brass, 27 × 24 cm / Signed: J. Kahane 1936
Inv. no. A-360.

131. Monk, 1931
Repoussé brass, 31 × 25.3 cm / Signed: Joa/Kahane/1931
Inv. no. A-361 / Purchased in 1948.

ARTUR SZYK
132. The Kalisz Statute, miniature no. 19, 1926 30
Printed on beige coated paper, gilded, 38.6 × 32.4 cm
Inv. no. A-1030/19 / Gift of CKŻP in 1950.

133. The Kalisz Statute, miniature no. 5, 1927
Printed on beige coated paper, gilded, 38.6 × 32.1 cm / Signed: Fait a Paris, en 1927, par arthur szyk, elumineur, humble eleve des grands elumineurs de France.
Inv. no. A-1030/5 / Gift of CKŻP in 1950.

MOJŻESZ LEJBOWSKI
134. Courtyard in Vilna

Oil on canvas fixed to a cardboard, 34.5 × 48 cm
Inv. no. A-1143.

RAFAEL LEWIN
135. Old Synagogue in Vilna, 1928
Oil on canvas, cardboard, 72.4 × 43.5 cm / Signed: רפאל לעווין
Inv. no. A-50 / Purchased in 1950. בישול תרפח 1928

RAFAŁ (RAFAEL) CHWOLES
136. Jewish Suburb in Vilna (Łukiszki), 1962
Monotype, 37 × 46.3 cm / Signed: 1962
Inv. no. A-715 / Purchased in 1963.

137. Tailors' Synagogue in Vilna, 1962
Monotype, 34.5 × 33.5 cm / Signed: R. Chvoles-62
Inv. no. A-198 / Purchased in 1963.

ADOLF BEHRMAN (BEHRMANN)
138. Jewish Water Carrier in the Market Place in Kazimierz Dolny
Mixed technique, 62.7 × 47.7 cm / Signed: Behrman
Inv. no. A-21 / Donated by Joint in 1950.

MAURYCY TRĘBACZ
139. Street in Kazimierz on the Vistula
Oil on cardboard, 57.7 × 72.5 cm / Signed: Maurycy Trębacz/Kazimierz
Inv. no. A-17 / Purchased in 1947.

SYMCHA (SIMON) BINEM TRACHTER
140. Landscape (Kazimierz Dolny), 1929
Oil on cardboard, 50 × 60 cm / Signed: S. Trachter 29
Inv. no. A-40 / Gift of Wiktor Ziółkowski in 1948.

MENASZE SEIDENBEUTEL
141. View of Kazimierz on the Vistula
Oil on canvas, 72 × 77.2 cm / Signed: Seidenbeutel M
Inv. no. A-25 / Purchased in 1960.

MARCIN KITZ
142. Small Town, 1928
Oil on canvas, cardboard, 36 × 31.2 cm / Signed: Kitz 928
Inv. no. A-691 / Purchased in 1949.

UNKNOWN PAINTER
143. Typical Characters from Kazimierz on the Vistula
Oil on canvas, 97.2 × 157.2 cm
Inv. no. A-156.

JÓZEF BADOWER
144. Water Carrier
Oil on canvas, 80.1 × 79.2 cm / Signed: J. Badower
Inv. no. A-443.

VINCENT (ICCHAK) BRAUNER
145. Water Carrier
Repoussé brass, 75 × 60 cm / Signed: V. Brauner
Inv. no. A-336 / Purchased in 1949.

MAREK SZWARC
146. Shepherd with a Lamb
Repoussé brass, 67 × 40 cm / Signed: Marek Szwarc
Inv. no. A-346 / Purchased in 1947.

ERNÖ ERB
147. At the Market
Oil on cardboard, 33 × 48 cm / Signed: E. Erb
Inv. no. A-94.

DAWID (DANIEL) GREIFENBERG (GRAJFENBERG)
148. Stream
Oil on canvas, 60 × 81.4 cm / Signed: greifenberg
Inv. no. A-20 / Donated by the Ministry of Culture and Art in 1949.

149. Small Town
Oil on canvas, 57 × 77.2 cm / Signed: greifenberg
Inv. no. A-74 / Donated by the Ministry of Culture and Art in 1949.

NATAN KORZEŃ
150. Cottages
Oil on cardboard, 69.4 × 80.3 cm / Signed: N. Korzeń
Inv. no. A-417 / Purchased in 1949.

HENRYK (HERSZ) RABINOWICZ
151. Ruins of a House
Oil on canvas, 55.7 × 65.3 cm / Signed: Rabinowicz H.
Inv. no. A-44 / Purchased in 1948.

SAMUEL FINKELSTEIN
152. Houses by the Water, 1930
Oil on canvas, 53.2 × 63 cm / Signed: Sam. Finkelstein 1930
Inv. no. A-289.

HENRYK LEWENSZTADT
153. Zakopane
Pastel, 42.8 × 60.5 cm / Signed: H. Lewensztadt
Inv. no. A-827 / Purchased in 1961.

SAMUEL HIRSZENBERG
154. Rural Landscape in Winter
Oil on canvas, 84.3 × 106.5 cm / Signed: S. Hirszenberg
Inv. no. A-700.

ARTUR MARKOWICZ
155. Brügge: Street in Sunlight, 1920
Pastel on cardboard, 49 × 63.5 cm / Signed: Markowicz/Brugge 1920
Inv. no. A-55 / Purchased in 1948.

ABRAHAM NEUMANN
156. Kalwaria Zebrzydowska, 1917
Pastel on cardboard, 68.6 × 97.5 cm / Signed: 1917 A. Neumann
Inv. no. A-6 / Purchased in 1947.

LEON ROZENBLUM (ROSENBLUM)
157. Winter Landscape
Oil on canvas, 69.7 × 91.7 cm / Signed: Leon Rosenblum
Inv. no. A-23 / Purchased in 1949.

NATAN SZPIGEL (SPIGEL)
158. Before the Cottage
Varnished watercolour on cardboard, 38 × 55 cm / Signed: Natan Szpigel
Inv. no. A-192.

HENRYK CYTRYN
159. Boy with a Cart, 1939
Oil on canvas, 66 × 74.5 cm / Signed: Cytryn 39
Inv. no. A-293.

HENRYK GOTLIB
160. Breton Landscape: On the Seashore, 1929 (?)
Oil on canvas, 54.9 × 74.3 cm / Signed: Henri Gotlib
Inv. no. A-18 / Purchased in 1947.

EMIL SCHINAGEL (SZINAGEL, SINAGEL)
161. Pension
Oil on canvas, 64.4 × 80 cm / Signed: Sinagel
Inv. no. A-53.

162. In the Cab
Oil on canvas, 54.3 × 65.5 cm / Signed: Szinagel
Inv. no. A-46 / Purchased in 1948.

ADOLF BEHRMAN (BEHRMANN)
163. Eastern Landscape, 1933
Oil on canvas fixed to a hardboard, 66.2 × 46.3 cm / Signed: Behrmann 33
Inv. no. A-411.

GIZELA HUFNAGLÓWNA-KLIMASZEWSKA-ARCTOWA
164. Apiary (Bee-hives), 1931
Oil on canvas, 68.5 × 58.2 cm / Signed: Gizela Hufnaglówna 931
Inv. no. A-394.

BERTA (BIMA) GRÜNBERG
165. Landscape
Oil on canvas, 50 × 60 cm / Signed: Grüberg
Inv. no. A-288 / Gift of Jonasz Stern in 1951.

SASZA (SZAJE) BLONDER (ANDRÉ BLONDEL)
166. Landscape with Houses
Oil on cardboard, 39.5 × 47.3 cm / Signed: Blonder
Inv. no. A-245 / Purchased in 1951.

ANIELA CUKIERÓWNA
167. View of St. Casimir's Convent from Okólnik Street, 1933
Colour woodcut, 24.5 × 29.7 cm / Signed: 20 IX 33 Aniela Cukierówna
Inv. no. A-736 / Purchased in 1960.

ADAM (ABRAHAM) HERSZAFT
168. Sicily
Etching, 15.8 × 23.1 cm / Signed: Adam Herszaft – Sycylja
Inv. no. A-799 / Purchased in 1950.

FISZEL ZYLBERBERG
169. Cello Player, 1934
Wood engraving, 15 × 10.8 cm / Signed: F. Zylberberg 1934
Inv. no. A-628 / Purchased in 1959.

MOSZE BERNSTEIN
170. Klezmer, 1982
Lithograph, 50 × 35.5 cm / Signed: מ. ברנשטיין 82
Inv. no. A-1369 / Gift of the artist in 1983.

EFRAIM AND MENASZE SEIDENBEUTEL
171. Still-life with Flowers
Oil on cardboard, 68 × 56.5 cm / Signed: Seidenbeutel
Inv. no. A-71 / Purchased in 1960.

FISZEL ZYLBERBERG (ZBER)
172. Still-life, 1933
Oil on canvas, 84 × 87 cm / Signed: F. Zylberberg 1933
Inv. no. A-159.

FELIKS FRYDMAN
173. Still-life
Watercolour on paper, 43.5 × 57 cm / Signed: Frydman
Inv. no. A-38 / Purchased in 1949.

ELIASZ KANAREK
174. Idyll, c. 1931
Oil, collage on canvas, 100.5 × 78.3 cm / Signed: E. Kanarek
Inv. no. A-1 / Donated by the Ministry of Culture and Art in 1949.

EFRAIM AND MENASZE SEIDENBEUTEL
175. Girl with a Pigeon in a Cage
Oil on canvas, 80.5 × 65.8 cm / Signed: Seidenbeutel
Inv. no. A-445.

HENRYK BERLEWI
176. Chonon and Leah, poster to *Dybbuk*, 1921
Lithograph, 29.8 × 26.2 cm / Signed: Dybuk. H. Berlewi 1921
Inv. no. A-108 / Donated by Joint in 1950.

ZYGMUNT MENKES
177. By the Well (Biblical Scene), 1923
Oil on canvas, 97 × 52 cm / Signed: Menkes 1923
Inv. no. A-182.

HUGO STEINER-PRAG
178. Golem, from the series *The Golem: A Prague Fantasy*, 1916
Lithograph, 15.5 × 14.9 cm / Signed: H.ST.
Inv. no. A-1031/2 / Purchased in 1961.

179. Alchemists' Street (Golden Street), from the series *The Golem: A Prague Fantasy*, 1916
Lithograph, 15.5 × 14.9 cm / Signed: Hugo Steiner-Prag 1916
Inv. no. A-1031/21 / Purchased in 1961.

BRUNO SCHULZ
180. Self-portrait with Stanisław Weingarten, 1921
Pencil, 24 × 31 / Signed: Bruno Schulz 1921
Inv. no. A-739.

181. Sadistic Women, 1919
Pencil, 29 × 40 cm / Signed: Bruno Schulz 1919
Inv. no. A-461 / Purchased in 1947.

182. Grotesque: Barrel Organ Player in the Courtyard, 1936
Ink, 16.2 × 19.9 cm / Signed: Bruno Schulz 1936
Inv. no. A-514 / Purchased in 1947.

183. By the Sick Bed, 1926
Ink and pencil, 14.5 × 16.5 cm / Signed: Bruno Schulz 1926
Inv. no. A-1399 / Gift of Ernestyna Podhorizer-Sandel in 1984.

JAN GOTARD
184. Fairy-tale about Cinderella, 1937
Oil on hardboard, 120 × 200 cm / Signed: Jan Gotard/1937
Inv. no. A-168 / Donated by the Ministry of Culture and Art in 1949.

185. Girl in a White Hat
Oil on hardboard, 49 × 54 cm / Signed: Gotard
Inv. no. A-1070 / Purchased in 1948.

186. Fortune-teller, 1933
Oil on hardboard, 99.5 × 89.5 cm
Inv. no. A-1072 / In the ŻIH Museum since 1949.

HENRYK GOTLIB
187. Study of a Woman Wearing a Hat, 1923
Oil on canvas, 55.5 × 46 cm / Signed: Henri Gotlib 23
Inv. no. A-81 / Purchased in 1946.

RAJMUND KANELBA (KANELBAUM)
188. Female Study
Oil on canvas, 65 × 54 cm / Signed: Kanelba
Inv. no. A-1067 / Purchased in 1948.

NATAN ALTMAN
189. Portrait of a Woman (Mrs. Braun), 1900
Oil on canvas, 75.6 × 58.3 cm / Signed: Altman 1900
Inv. no. A-306 / In the ŻIH Museum since 1948.

LEOPOLD HOROWITZ
190. Portrait of Helena Hermanówna, 1881
Oil on canvas, 123 × 96 cm / Signed: Horowitz 1881
Inv. no. A-155 / In the ŻIH Museum since 1948.

Helena Hermanówna (c. 1860–1916), dancer and singer. Made her début as a singer in the Grand Theatre in Warsaw in 1879. Also appeared in Lvov, St. Petersburg, Moscow, Berlin and Milan. Lost her voice as a result of a protracted illness and gave up her career.

LEOPOLD GOTTLIEB
191. Portrait of Dr. Ber Kupczyk, c. 1907
Oil on canvas, 115 × 85 cm / Signed: L. Gottlieb
Inv. no. A-160 / Purchased in 1948.

BER (Bernard) Kupczyk b. Działoszyce, 1870, d. Cracow, 1941
Neurologist, graduate of the Jagiellonian University in Cracow in 1894. Before the Second World War, owner of the "Salus" psychiatric clinic in Cracow. One of the founders of the Hebrew secondary school in Cracow.

JERZY (GEORG) MERKEL
192. Portrait of Artur Markowicz, 1906
Pastel, 54.2 × 42.8 cm.
Inv. no. A-63 / Purchased in 1947.

ROMAN KRAMSZTYK
193. Portrait of a Man, 1928
Oil on canvas, 98.3 × 66.5 cm / Signed: Kramstyk Anno/Domini/1928
Inv. no. A-2 / Purchased in 1947.

194. Man in a Bowler Hat
Oil on canvas, 99.3 × 81 cm / Signed: Kramstyk
Inv. no. A-1068 / Purchased in 1948.

IZRAEL LEJZEROWICZ
195. Portrait of a Man, 1930
Oil on canvas, 69 × 54.6 cm / Signed: I. Lejzerowicz 30
Inv. no. A-47 / Purchased in 1949.

STANISŁAWA CENTNERSZWEROWA
196. Portrait of an Old Woman, 1941
Oil on canvas, 91.5 × 72.8 cm / Signed: S Cent 41
Inv. no. A-36 / Gift of Dr. Czajkowska in 1951.

SAMUEL FINKELSTEIN
197. Self-portrait
Oil on canvas, 84.7 × 62.8 cm.
Inv. no. A-57.

EMIL ORLIK
198. Ernst Haeckel, 1901
Etching, 20.4 × 16.1 cm / Signed: Orlik 1901 Insulinde, 53 Ernst Haeckel.
Inv. no. B-443/48 / Donated by the Ministry of Culture and Art in 1951.

MAX LIEBERMANN
199. Portrait of Hermann Cohen
Etching, 23 × 16.3 cm / Signed: M. Liebermann
Inv. no. B-443/32 / Donated by the Ministry of Culture and Art in 1951.

Hermann Cohen (1842–1918), professor of philosophy at the university of Marburg (1872–1912), founder of the Marburg school of Neo-Kantianism.

LEON BAKST
200. Portrait of Levitan, 1899
Lithograph, 36.6 × 32 cm / Signed: Bakst
Inv. no. A-756 / Purchased in 1948.

Izaak Levitan (1861–1900), Russian painter.

GELA SEKSZTAJN
201. Self-portrait
Charcoal, 22.8 × 17 cm
Inv. no. A-897 / Acquired from Ringelblum's Archives in 1946.

JÓZEF ŚLIWNIAK
202. Head of a Woman
Repoussé copper, 40 × 27.5 cm
Inv. no. A-356 / Purchased in 1949.

MAREK SZWARC
203. Portrait of Bergelson, 1925
Metalwork, 34.2 × 39 cm / Signed: Marek Szwarc, Paris 1925 בערגעלסאן
Inv. no. A-355 / Purchased in 1948.

HENRYK (HENOCH) BARCIŃSKI
204. John the Baptist, 1919
Linocut, 19.8 × 19 cm / Signed: Henoch Barciński חנוך בארצינסקי
(John the Baptist) „יוחנן המטביל" / dedicated to
Mojżesz Broderson] געווידמעט משה בראָדערזאָן
ŻIH Library, inv. no. 05796.

WILHELM WACHTEL
205. Christ in the Pogrom District, plate from the graphic series *Farewell to Galus*
Lithograph, 43.2 × 52 cm / Signed: WW
Inv. no. A-859/24, 25.

HENRYK KUNA
206. Bust of Felicja Winawerowa
Plaster, 45 cm / Signed: H. Kuna
Deposit no. 1.

KONSTANTY LASZCZKA
207. Head of a Jew
Patinated bronze, 47.5 cm / Signed: K. Laszczka
Inv. no. A-996 / Purchased in 1949.

RYSZARD MOSZKOWSKI
208. Portrait of a woman with a shawl on her head
Bronze, 35 cm / Signed: RM
Inv. no. A-997 / Gift of the artist's mother in 1951.

209. Nude Boy, 1943
Bronze, 93,2 cm / Signed: RM 43
Inv. no. A-1011 / Gift of the artist's mother in 1951.

JULIA RINGEL-KEILOWA
210. Statue of the Actress Elżbieta Barszczewska, 1937
Pear wood, 183 cm / Signed: Julia Keilowa 1937
Inv. no. A-1010 / In the ŻIH Museum since 1951.

Elżbieta Barszczewska (1913–87), actress, from 1934 appeared in the Polski and National theatres in Warsaw, also a popular film star, e.g. *The Borderline, Girls from Nowolipki Street,* and *The Leper.*

HELENA GŁOGOWSKA
211. Motherhood, c. 1937
Bronze, 63 cm / Signed: G H; L Krank i T Łempicki/Warszawa
Deposit no. 4.

MAGDALENA GROSS
212. Head of a Woman
Bronze, 35 cm / Signed: MAGDALENA GROSS
Inv. no. A-1018 / Purchased in 1948.

ROMAN KRAMSZTYK
213. Head of a Girl Wearing a Turban
Bronze, 36 cm / Signed: R. Kramsztyk, odlewał/L. Kranc/Warszawa [cast by L. Kranc/Warsaw]
Inv. no. A-989 / Purchased in 1961.

GELA SEKSZTAJN
214. Portrait of a Girl
Watercolour, 78 × 45 cm / Signed: G. Seksztajn
Inv. no. A-28 / Acquired from Ringelblum's Archives in 1946.

HERSZ SCHILLIS (SZYLIS)
215. Ghetto Jew, 1942
Charcoal, 68.5 × 50 cm / Signed: H. Schilis, Litzmannstadt, Getto 1942.
Inv. no. A-432.

MACIEJ LACHUR
216. Execution, 1957
Oil on canvas, 100 × 70 cm / Signed: M. Lachur 57.
Inv. no. A-1036 / In the ŻIH Museum since 1963.

MAREK OBERLÄNDER
217. Kol Nidre, 1955
Oil on canvas, 81 × 100 cm.
Inv. no. A-447 / Gift of the artist in 1961.

HELENA GAŁKOWSKA
218. Candleholders, 1978
Woollen tapestry, 245 × 145 cm, woven by S. Władyga
Inv. no. A-1214 / Gift of Izaak and Pepi Levin of the US.

LIST OF ARTISTS

Numbers refer to illustrations and Catalogue (in brackets)

Illustrations

Torah shield (Heb. *tas*) forms part of the ornament adorning the Torah scroll. The custom of decorating the Torah scroll in this way is said to go back to the late Middle Ages and served the practical purpose of indicating the place where the scroll was to be unwound, which meant that, whenever more than one scroll was used, one did not have to lose time searching for the right lines. For the Talmud teaches that no time should be lost rewinding the Torah in the synagogue, but instead another scroll prepared for the occasion must be used. And indeed the majority of Torah shields have, in their lower section, a small box with plates specifying the festival and occasion on which the scroll is to be utilized. There are also breastplates without such boxes. Since these are on the whole very modest, made of base metals, it seems that they come from poor synagogues which could not afford more than one scroll of the Law. The shield form is also sometimes associated with the breastplate worn by the High Priest (Ex. xxviii, 15–30, xxxix, 8–21).

1. Torah shield, Poland,
   18th cent.

2. Torah shield, Wrocław, 18th cent.
3. Torah shield, Berlin, first quarter of the 19th cent.
4. Torah shield, Wrocław, 1762–72.

5. Torah shield, Płock?, 1857.
6. Torah shield, Berlin, second half of the 19th cent.

7. Torah shield, Germany?, 19th cent.
8. Torah shield, Germany, 1893.

It is customary to top the Torah scrolls with a crown (*Heb. keter*) and pairs of finials called rimmonim (pomegranates in Hebrew). The crown is meant to underline the holiness and significance of the Torah, as well as the particular veneration due to it. The custom of adorning the Law with a crown is generally believed to be associated with a passage from the *Pirke Avoth* (iv, 17): "Rabbi Simeon used to say: There are three crowns: the crown of the Torah, the crown of priesthood and the crown of royalty, but the crown of the good name is superior to them all"*.

Instead of the crown the Torah scroll may be embellished with rimmonim of various shapes, usually in the form of pomegranates or crowns. The pomegranate, a plant characteristic of biblical flora, is frequently mentioned in the Old Testament, and often appeared as a decorative motif in biblical times and later. The crowns of the columns in the Temple of Solomon were adorned with bronze cast pomegranates hanging from chains. Sometimes the rimmonim are called *azei hayyim* or "the trees of life", the name also applied to the rolls on which the Torah scrolls are wound, and derived from the biblical metaphor: "She is a tree of life to them that lay hold upon her: and happy is every one that retaineth her" (Prov. iii, 18). The crowns and rimmonim were always decorated with bells, and the origin of this custom can be traced to the Pentateuch (Ex. xxviii, 3–35). According to biblical precepts the lower hem of the high priest's robes had to be adorned with pomegranates and golden bells so that he could be heard whenever he entered and departed behind the curtain which screened the Most Holy Place where the Ark stood. A similar role is performed by bells in the synagogue, which are sounded each time the Torah is produced from the aron ha-kodesh.

* Pirke Avot (Ethics of the Fathers) or the ninth tractate of the fourth order of the Talmud entitled Nezikin (Damages), which is a collection of moral and religious precepts uttered by the sages.

9. Torah crown, Berlin, late 19th cent.
10. Torah crown, Poland, 1853.

11. Rimmon, Germany, late 19th cent.
12. Rimmon, Greece, 19th cent.
13. Rimmonim, Greece?, 19th/20th cent.

Torah pointer (Heb. *yad,* meaning literally hand) is a wand, its handle having various shapes, usually ending with a representation of the hand with its index finger sticking out.

It is generally accepted that the custom of using the yad originated in the special treatment which had to be given to the Torah, this being a holy scripture which must not be profaned by touching it with the bare finger. To trace the lines therefore a special pointer was used during readings in the synagogues. The first *yadayim* were probably produced in Germany in the 16th century.

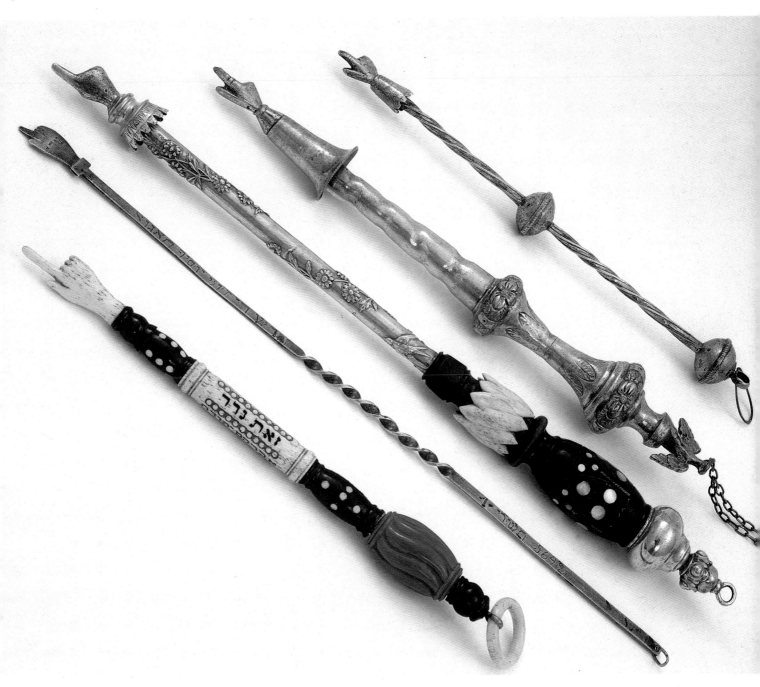

15. Torah pointers (from top cats. 16–20).

14. Rimmonim, Salonika, 19th/20th cent. (cat. 14).
    Rimmonim, Greece?, 19th/20th cent. (cat. 15).

16. Torah pointers (from top cats. 21–24).

The Torah binder (Heb. *hitul le-Torah*) is a long, narrow, ornamented strip of cloth (11–24 cm wide and 180–400 cm long), adorned with inscriptions in Hebrew. The binder was put round the scrolls of the Torah and in turn was covered by the mantle. This custom, unknown to Polish Jews, originated among the German Ashkenazi Jews in the 16th century and subsequently spread to the other countries of central and western Europe.

The scroll of the Torah is first bound with a strip of cloth (between 5 and 7.6 cm wide), called *gartl* (to bind) in Yiddish and *avnet* (belt) in Hebrew, which is occasionally embroidered with dedicatory inscriptions. The Torah binder is a variant of this *gartl*. It is called *wimpel* (streamer) in German, *bindel* in Yiddish, and *hitul* (bandage or nappy) in modern Hebrew. The Polish name – meaning swaddling clothes – refers to the material from which it was usually made – the swaddling clothes of baby boys used during the ceremony of circumcision.

The binder was usually composed of three or four strips joined together. Along its length there was a Hebrew inscription in two parts. The first part consisted of the names of the boy and his father, and the date of birth; the second was an excerpt from the prayer said during the ceremony of circumcision – that the new born should grow up to the Torah (learning), the *huppah* (marriage) and *ma'asim tovim* (good deeds). These inscriptions were adorned with flowers, animals, birds, geometrical motifs, representations of the unwound scroll of the Torah and a realistic or symbolic scene of betrothal under the *huppah*. The motifs employed were often inspired by the baby's name and sign of the zodiac. The binder was usually made by the new born's mother or other female relations. When the little boy (at three or four) first visited the synagogue he brought his binder as an offering to the Torah. At his *bar mitzvah* the Torah he read from was clothed in his binder.

A different type of binder was used in Alsace and in Italy. Such binders, which had nothing to do with the birth of a boy, were called *mappah* (Heb. for table cloth), and were made of various kinds of fabric, usually patterned silk. They were bequeathed mostly by women and the inscriptions that adorned them were completely different from the German ones. They usually consisted of the name of the donor and the reason for the bequest, for example in commemoration of the late father, grandfather or husband, in honour of a marriage, in thanksgiving for numerous offspring, in the hope that the husband or father would live long, or on the occasion of the construction of a synagogue or some other important event.

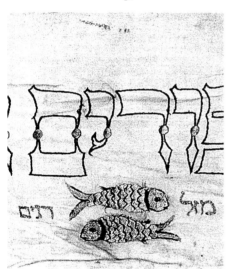  

17. Torah binder, Germany?, 1754 (cat. 25).

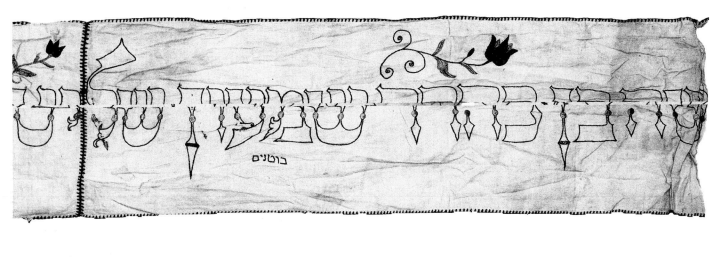

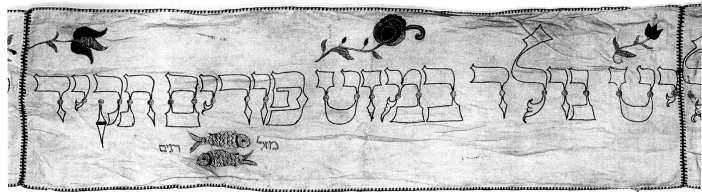

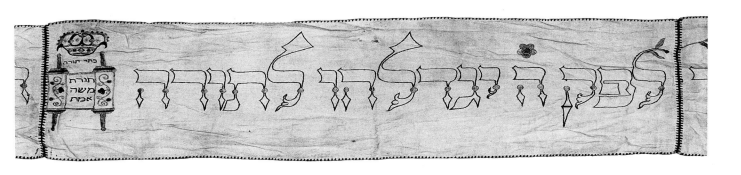

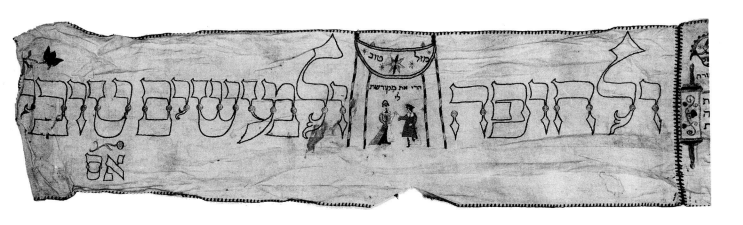

18. Torah binder, Germany?, 1861 (cat. 26).

The Torah mantle (Heb. *meil*) served to protect and decorate the Torah scrolls kept in the aron ha-kodesh (Talmud, Shabbat 133b). Different colours could be used during the year, with the exception of New Year (Rosh ha-Shana) and the Day of Atonement (Yom Kippur) when white mantles were obligatory (at the same time a white curtain was hung in front of the aron ha-kodesh). The inscriptions adorning the mantles usually referred to the names of the donors.

The Sephardic Jews used, in addition to mantles, wooden or metal covers, richly ornamented.

19. Torah mantle, Germany?, 1896 (cat. 27).

קדש לה
זאת נדבה אשר
הפריש מתרומת
כספם היקר הר
יוסף משה חבר
היו ובנו היקר
מרדכי היו לכבוד
אביו ישלם ה
פעלם

שנת
5656

23. Torah mantle, Salonika, 1893 (cat. 31).

20. Torah mantle, Greece, second half of the 19th cent. (cat. 28).
21. Torah mantle, Greece, second half of the 19th cent. (cat. 29).
22. Torah mantle, Greece, 1896 (cat. 30).

The custom of hanging a curtain (Heb. *parokhet)* on the aron ha-kodesh* goes back to biblical times and God's injunctions concerning the furnishing of the first Sanctuary. The present parokhet corresponds to the veil which in the Tabernacle, and then in the Temple in Jerusalem, separated the Holy Place from the Holy of Holies occupied by the Ark of the Covenant with the tablets of the Decalogue (Ex. xxvi, 31–34; 2 Chron. iii, 14). Only the High Priest could go beyond the veil and even he could only do so once a year. This took place on Yom Kippur, or the Day of Atonement when the priest begged God for forgiveness for himself and the entire people of Israel (Lev. xvi, 1–34, xxiii, 26–32; Heb. ix, 7). The biblical parokhet hid from the faithful the Divine Presence, the Shekinah, which according to tradition dwelled among the cherubim that adorned the covering of the Ark of the Covenant.

The curtain may be of any colour, but on New Year (Rosh ha-Shana) and the Day of Atonement (Yom Kippur) white is obligatory**. The excellent workmanship of some surviving curtains indicates that they were produced by renowned craftsmen or manufacturers. Other parokhets, made of various assorted pieces of fabric, were usually the work of women of a given community. Each parokhet usually had a matching lambrequin (Heb. *kaporet)****. The latter word can be found in the Bible (Ex. xxv, 17–22) where it denotes a solid slab of gold (the propitiatory or mercy seat) with two cherubim at either end, which lay upon the Ark of the Covenant. The applying of this word to the lambrequin is in a sense a continuation of the biblical tradition. Also the decorating of the veils with two lions facing each other and supporting a crown – a motif typical of Jewish religious art – is particularly appropriate here. Lions are regarded as the symbol of the tribe of Judah but here they rather correspond to the cherubim from the original kaporet which covered the Ark of the Covenant. In the Old Testament and in rabbinical literature, the cherubim are represented as human beings or animals (Ezek. xii, 18–19).

The inscriptions placed on the parokhets are usually of a dedicatory character, or else consist of quotations from the Bible and excerpts from prayers. In the 18th century representations of the furnishing of the original Tabernacle and the Temple in Jerusalem became popular.

---

* Aron ha-kodesh (holy box or ark) is a niche built into the eastern wall of the synagogue or else a case put there, where the scrolls of the Torah are kept. The name comes from the biblical Ark of the Covenant. According to Sephardic tradition, the curtain is usually placed behind the door of the aron ha-kodesh.

** During these festivals Jews atone for and cleanse themselves of their sins. The white colour, which was also obligatory in clothes, was the symbol of purity.

*** The root of the Hebrew word *kaporet* has two meanings: to atone and to cover.

24. Torah Ark curtain, Prussia–Silesia, 1774 (cat. 32).

25. Torah Ark curtain with valance, Prussia–Silesia, 1783 (cat. 33).

26. Torah Ark curtain, Poland?, late 17th cent. (cat. 34).

27. Torah Ark curtain, Germany, 1872 (cat. 35).
28. Torah Ark curtain, Turkey, late 19th cent. (cat. 36).
29. Cover for the cantor's desk, Turkey, late 19th cent. (cat. 37).

Candlesticks for one candle, single or in pairs – unlike other religious objects such as Hanukkah lamps and spice boxes whose use was ascribed to one religion only, Judaism – served both Jews and Christians, believers and non-believers. Hence their design usually reflected current styles in art and lacked the symbols characteristic of Jewish religious art. Sometimes the only indication that they were used by Jews are inscriptions added later, or what we know of their history, and only in exceptional cases do the ornamentations tell us anything, e.g. palm trees or vines and grapes, although these symbols do not exclude non-Jewish owners.

Jews lit candles to observe holidays, weddings, anniversaries of deaths and above all the most festive day – the beginning of the Sabbath, when the lady of the house lit two candles (which according to one interpretation were meant to recall two commandments given by God in the Pentateuch: "Remember the sabbath day", Ex. xx, 8, and "Keep the sabbath day", Deut. v, 12), and recited a special blessing over them. Hence such pairs of candleholders are frequently referred to as Sabbath candles.

30. Pair of candlesticks, Vienna, 1840 (cat. 38).
    Cups (from left cats. 55–56).
31. Pair of candlesticks, Vienna, late 19th cent. (cat. 39).

32. Candlestick , Warsaw, after 1852, (cat. 40).
33. Candlesticks, Warsaw, 20th cent. (from left cats. 41–42).
34. Pair of candlesticks, Silesia?, 19th cent. (cat. 43).

Goblets, cups and beakers, those imposing and made of precious metals, usually silver, were used above all on the Sabbath and various other festivals. Before a festive meal, they were filled with wine (traditionally red) and the prayer called Kiddush (Heb. for sanctification) was said over them to sanctify the beginning of the Sabbath or festival. When there was no wine, the Kiddush prayer was recited over two loaves of bread. Kiddush is a prayer going back to the times before the Great Assembly*, and may be also sung in the synagogue, mainly for travellers – so that they too can take part in the full liturgy of the festival (in Israel the Kiddush prayer is never recited in the synagogue).

Like candlesticks, cups and goblets usually formed part of ordinary table sets. They reflected the currently prevailing style and only rarely (unless they were made to a special order) did they feature ornaments typical of Jewish religious art. However, festive cups and goblets were frequently additionally adorned later with excerpts from prayers prescribed for the given festival or dedicatory inscriptions, the latter, apart from cases where the history of a given item is known, usually being the only mark enabling us to correctly classify the object. It was common in the late 19th and early 20th centuries in Eastern Europe for silver cups of various sizes to be used (the largest for the master of the house and the smallest for the children). Year after year the same patterns and motifs recurred, mostly plant and geometrical ornaments and architectural views of Jerusalem and other holy places in the Promised Land. Cups and goblets with no special inscriptions referring to the festival they served were probably also used during other occasions, whenever it was necessary to empty a cup of wine that had been blessed, for example during the ritual of circumcision, a wedding or other festive meals called *seuda*.

Among Jews, wine, as well as bread, played a particular role. It was more than just an ordinary, everyday drink. At one stage offerings of wine were made in the Temple. With the end of the Temple rite (70 A.D.) some elements of the ancient liturgy were adopted in an altered form for use in the domestic and synagogal rites. When food is being blessed, this is done in a general way, with no distinction as to the kind of food. This is not true of wine and bread which both call for a special benediction.

* The Great Assembly (Heb. *Knesset ha-Gdola*), a special council formed for the purpose of the correct interpretation of the Law, later known as the Sanhedrin.

35. Cups and goblets (from left cats. 44–48).

36. Goblet, Poland?, 1890 (cat. 49).

37. Goblet, Cracow, 1922–39 (cat. 50).
38. Goblet, Moscow, 1875 (cat. 51).
39. Synagogal goblet, Berlin, 1900 (cat. 52).

The spice box (Heb. *besamim,* Yid. *bsumim-büchse* or *shmekier,* in Poland known as *balsaminka*) was used at home and in the synagogue at the end of the Sabbath, during the Havdalah ceremony. During Havdalah (Heb. separation), which symbolizes the division between a holiday and other days of the week, the candle light, wine and spices are blessed using prescribed prayers. The shapes of besamims vary. The earliest and most popular form, which appeared first in the Middle Ages, is that of a tower. It is said to be derived from Christian liturgical vessels, e.g. censers, reliquaries and monstrances, or else from decorative architectural motifs employed in mediaeval town buildings where spices brought from the East were stored. There are also besamims in the forms of fruit, blossoms, fish or toys. Besamims were usually made of silver or base metals, occasionally of wood. Small, pear-shaped besamims on a chain were used by travellers.

The earliest references to besamims come from Germany and date from the 12th century. The ceremony of Havdalah is very old and goes back to the 5th-4th century B.C. Some trace the origins of the custom of smelling aromatic herbs on the Sabbath evening to practices dating from Hellenic times when after meals special spices were burnt to remove offensive odours. Others believe that the aroma of Sabbath herbs strengthens and inures the spirit before the approaching troubles and hardships of the week, or else that it is a compensation for the loss of the extra soul which accompanies each Jew during the Sabbath and leaves him when the holiday is over.

As for the term aromatic spices, this does not appear in the Bible where the term incense is used, but comes from talmudic and Midrash literature. From biblical times till the destruction of the second Temple in 70 A.D., incense – either by itself or together with offerings of food (e.g. added on each Sabbath to shewbread, Lev. xxiv, 7–8) was used to honour God. It was specially prepared and destined exclusively to be burnt in the Temple, and only priests were allowed to perform this ceremony. With the end of the Temple cult, offerings were no longer made, including incense offerings, and their place was taken by prayers. It is possible that the blessing of aromatic herbs in the Havdalah ("Praised art thou, Eternal, Our Lord, King of the Universe / who createst diverse kinds of spices") commemorates those times, just like other components of the Sabbath ritual, such as the presence of two loaves of bread on the table in memory of the shewbread offered in the Temple.

40. Spice box and cup (from left cats. 67, 53).
41. Spice box and goblet (from left cats. 68, 54).

42. Spice boxes (from left cats. 57–59).
43. Spice boxes (from left cats. 60–61).
44. Spice boxes (from left cats. 62–64).
45. Spice boxes (from left cats. 65–66).

Containers for etrogs are meant to preserve the fruit of etrog during the Sukkoth feast, lasting for eight days beginning with the 15th of Tishri, which usually corresponds to late September and early October. Originally a harvest festival marking the autumn ingathering of grain and fruit, it coincided with the biblical holiday prescribed by the Pentateuch and celebrated to commemorate the forty-year-long march of the Jews through the desert from their Egyptian captivity to the Promised Land. As the Old Testament commands: "And ye shall take you on the first day the boughs of goodly trees, branches of palm trees, and the boughs of thick trees, and willows of the brook; and ye shall rejoice before the LORD your God seven days" (Lev. xxiii, 40), the symbols that are carried round the synagogue during the festival are a branch of the palm tree (*lulov*), three sprigs of myrtle (*hadassim*) and two boughs of willow (*aravot*) in the right hand (the whole bunch customarily called *lulov*), and an etrog (a species of citrus fruit) in the left hand. According to the generally accepted interpretation, the four plants symbolize four groups of people – depending on the role the Torah performs in their lives. The etrog, a fruit that has a pleasant smell and taste, represents the most perfect people, those who know the Torah, follow faithfully its precepts and perform good deeds. The etrog chosen for Sukkoth has to be fine and unblemished. The Sephardic Jews preferred round and thick fruit, Hungarian Jews were in favour of oval fruit with smooth skin, while Galician Jews sought specimens with uneven, porous skin. Some believe that the most suitable fruit is one with a *pittom,* or a small growth at the bottom, preferably in a stright line from the base. European communities imported their etrogs from the Island of Corfu.

In Israel the etrog is wrapped in cotton cloth brought specially from Bangladesh, so that it keeps its freshness and smell. Containers for preserving the etrog are rare and it seems that the custom is not all that old. Such containers often have the shape of the fruit in question, and in such cases their function is obvious, but it also frequently happened that other items, for example, sugar bowls, were adapted to this purpose.

46. Etrog container, Moscow, 1844 (cat. 69).

Hanukkah lamps with eight vessels to hold oil or candles are lit on the feast of Hanukkah which extends for eight days from the 25th of the month of *Kislev* to the 2nd of the month of *Tevet,* corresponding to the latter half of December. Hanukkah commemorates the victory of Judah Maccabee over the Syrian king Antiochus IV Epiphanes (175–163) in 164 (1 Macc. iv, 59; 2 Macc. x, 7–8). The revolt broke out in protest against restrictions imposed by the Syrian ruler who forbade the practice of the Jewish religion and turned the Temple in Jerusalem into a pantheon of Greek gods. After the Maccabees' victory the Temple was ceremoniously re-dedicated (Heb. *Hanukkah*) – hence the name of the festival. During Hanukkah, one cruse of oil or one candle is lit after sundown on the first day, two on the second, and so on for each evening of the festival. The candles are lit from left to right but inserted from right to left. Unlike lamps lit on the Sabbath or other holidays, the light of the Hanukkah lamp serves exclusively to add lustre to the festive character of the occasion and cannot be used for any practical purposes*. For this reason, there is usually an additional light (Heb. *Shammash* or servant), from which all the remaining lights are lit. Some lamps have another spout – which gives a total of ten (sometimes there are as many as twelve) – which is kindled on the Sabbath falling during the Hanukkah festival, a time when the lamp performs a double role. In the Talmudic period and later, Hanukkah lamps were hung in the windows or outside the entrance: in the latter case on the left door post, with the mezuzah on the right post – hence many of them have a back wall. There are also Hanukkah lamps in the form of nine-branched menorahs or rectangular cases with lids, the latter used by travellers. The spouts of Hanukkah lamps have the shape of jugs, vessels or separate compartments and are adapted above all to burning oil. This tradition is meant to recall the fact that when the Temple in Jerusalem was re-dedicated, oil was used to light the seven-branched candelabrum.

* The blessing uttered when the Hanukkah lamp is lit includes the following words: "Through all the days of Hanukkah these lights remain sacred and cannot be used, but only looked at."

47. Hanukkah lamp, Poland, 19th/20th cent. (cat. 70).   48. Hanukkah lamp, Silesia?, first half of the 19th cent. (cat. 71).

49. Hanukkah lamp, Eastern Europe, early 19th ce
(cat. 72).
50. Hanukkah lamp, Warsaw, 1871 (cat. 73).

51. Hanukkah lamp, Warsaw,
    second half of the 19th cent. (cat. 74).
52. Hanukkah lamp, Warsaw, 19th cent. (cat. 75).

53. Hanukkah lamp, Eastern Europe, 18th/19th cent. (cat. 76).
54. Hanukkah lamp, Poland, 19th/20th cent. (cat. 77).
55. Hanukkah lamp, Poland?, 19th cent. (cat. 78).
56. Hanukkah lamp, Warsaw, second half of the 19th cent.

The scroll of Esther (Heb. Megillat Esther) is the biblical Book of Esther written on parchment. The Book of Esther tells the story of the miraculous rescue of Jews in Persia in the 5th century B.C. by the wife of King Ahasverus of Persia, Queen Esther, who frustrated the designs to slay the Jewish people concocted by Haman, the prime minister of the Persian ruler. Haman determined by lot (in Hebrew *pur*) the 13th of Adar as the day on which the Jews were to be slain. Hence the name of the festival, Purim, or the Feast of Lots, which is celebrated on the 14th and 15th of Adar*, usually corresponding to early March. The first *megilloth* according to the Old Testament were sent in the form of a letter describing the events and ordering the Jews to commemorate them (Esth. ix, 20).

The text of the Megillat must be hand-written in ink on parchment. Illuminated scrolls were used for domestic rites. Since in the Book of Esther there is no single reference to God, illustrations could be even produced by children. The Megillat read in synagogue was never illustrated. With the development of printing techniques, Megilloth were provided with copperplate or wood-engraved illustrations. From the copies in our possession it becomes obvious that *soferim,* or scribes, were not always gifted artists. Their drawings are often clumsy and awkward, especially their depictions of the human figure. Genre scenes inspired by the Bible and "purim" shows (*purimspils*), frequently with ideas coming from Midrash literature**, fail to convey the realities of the times described in the Book of Esther, and instead depict the events in settings dating from various epochs, e.g. in the convention of commedia dell'arte. Apart from illustrations inspired by the Book of Esther, Megilloth were embellished with decorative borders of guilloches (e.g. Italian Megilloth) or floral and plant motifs with images of birds and animals. Illustrators usually adhered to the canons and symbols obligatory in Jewish religious art, while as regards ornamental motifs they relied heavily on current styles and folk art. Occasionally, a Megillat may end or begin with the text of a blessing recited before and after the reading and the emblem of the country of origin.

The scrolls were kept on rolls, with smaller items in decorative cases, often of silver, with rich ornamentation. From these, the text was gradually produced during its reading with the help of a special crank. The Megillat Esther is read at home and in the synagogue twice, on the evening and on the following morning, after the first prayers.

* According to the Old Testament (Esth. IX, 18), the Feast of Lots was celebrated for the first time outside the walls of ancient Susa on the 14th of Adar and within its walls on the 15th. Hence in cities that were once surrounded with walls, e.g. Jerusalem, the day is customarily celebrated on the 15th of Adar, while elsewhere, e.g. in Tel Aviv, the feast is observed on the 14th.

** For example, the drawings showing the beheading of Queen Vashti or Haman's daughter pouring a bucket of dirt onto her father's head while he brings Mordecai, dressed in royal robes, round the municipal square.

57. Scroll of Esther, Złotów?, Złoczów?, first half of the 19th cent. (cat. 80).

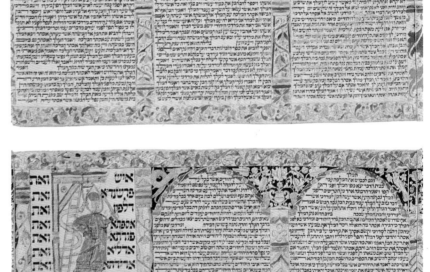

58. Esther Scroll cases (from top cats. 81–82).

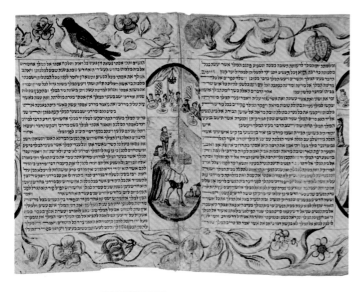

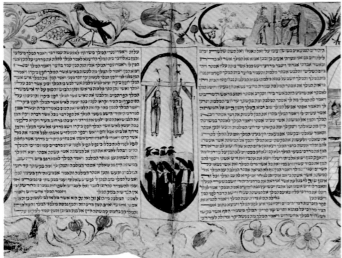

59. Scroll of Esther, Austria?, 18th/19th cent. (cat. 83).

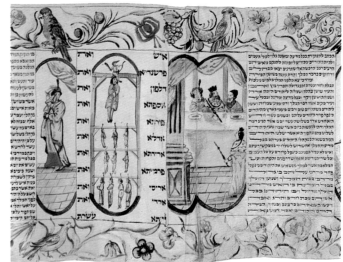

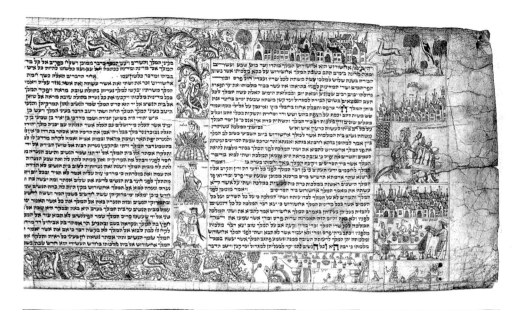

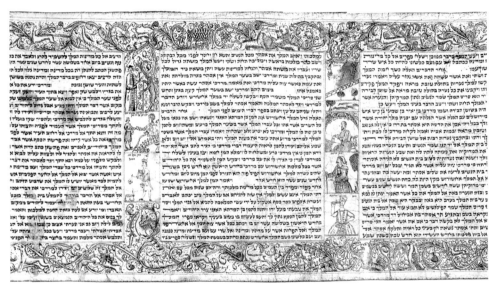

איש

ואת פרשנדתא
ואת דלפון
ואת אספתא
ואת פורתא
ואת אדליא
ואת ארידתא
ואת פרמשתא
ואת אריסי
ואת ארידי
ואת ויזתא
עשרת

ואת פרשנדתא
ואת דלפון
ואת אספתא
ואת פורתא
ואת אדליא
ואת ארידתא
ואת פרמשתא
ואת אריסי
ואת ארידי
ואת ויזתא
עשרת

The matzah bag (Yid. *matsetash*) was used during the feast of the Passover for keeping three pieces of matzot which according to the adopted tradition symbolized the caste division of the Jewish people into Priests, Levites and Israelites. The shape – usually an oval adapted to the shape of a loaf of matzah – and workmanship of such bags was reminiscent of pillow cases. Matzah bags were embellished with plant and flower ornaments and symbols of the feast of the Pesach – a representation of the Paschal lamb, seder cup and inscriptions explaining the order of the Seder feast. They were usually made by women at home.

61. Matzah bag, Łódź?, 1912 (cat. 85).

Seder plates were used during the Seder, a special meal on the first night of the Pesach. The Pesach, observed for seven days in Israel and eight days in the Diaspora, beginning with the 15th of the month of Nisan (March–April) during the first full moon following the spring solstice, commemorates the miraculous escape of the Israelites under the leadership of Moses from their slavery in Egypt. The Seder (meaning order in Hebrew), proceeds in accordance with a certain order. The symbolic foods, which are placed on the Seder table, are meant to remind the celebrants of their ancestors' hard lot during the Egyptian captivity and the night of their deliverance.

It is difficult to establish when the Seder as we know it today was held for the first time, though the custom undoubtedly has its roots in the night when the Jewish people prepared for the departure from Egypt, during which three of the seven dishes listed on the Seder plates were eaten: matzah, zeroa and maror (Ex. xii, 8). Matzah – or unleavened bread – recalls the haste with which the Israelites prepared their flight (Ex. xii, 8, xxiii, 15; Lev. xxiii, 4–8, Num. xxviii, 16–17, Deut. xvi, 3–4). Zeroa, a piece of roast meat containing a bone, is a reminder of the lamb killed and eaten during the night when they departed from Egypt (Ex. xii, 8, Deut. xvi, 5–7). Maror, or bitter herbs, symbolizes the bitterness of the Israelites' life in slavery in Egypt (Ex. xii, 8; Num. ix, 11). The remaining dishes, which the Old Testament does not mention, are: baytza, or a baked egg symbolizing holiday offerings made in the Temple and mourning after its loss; charoseth, or sweet pulp of nuts (almonds), apples, cinnamon and wine, which recalls the mortar (clay) produced by the Jews for Pharaoh; karpas, or green parsley or another vegetable (radishes, cucumbers, potatoes), dipped in brine, regarded as a symbol of the tears shed by the Israelites in their slavery (according to some this tradition goes back to the 1st-2nd century A.D., when each meal began with this appetizer)*; and chazeret, or a kind of bitter vegetables.

Since on the Pesach all leaven is strictly prohibited, a special set of dishes and cutlery should be used on this festival. Families that could not afford a separate dinner service, refrained from using pots and plates from materials having absorbent properties; the remaining dishes were sterilized and left for twenty-four hours, after which time they became *kosher,* that is, ready to be used.

* This ceremony symbolizes also the miracle of Red Sea crossing by Israelites.

62. Seder plate, Germany?,
    first half of the 19th cent.
    (cat. 86).
63. Plate, Jerusalem,
    1906–29 (cat. 87).

The washing of hands at home and in the synagogue may have either a ritual or a hygienic character. It is obligatory, for example, before meals when bread is served and before morning prayers when ablutions are accompanied by a special benediction called *Netilath yadayim*. After a meal, before the final prayer, hands are again washed symbolically, but without a benediction. The latter ceremony is called *maim acharonim* (the last waters) and is of a hygienic character. Similarly during the Seder feast – as we know from iconographic sources – the custom is to wash hands without a blessing before parsley dipped in brine is eaten. Hands are not washed through dipping them in water, but by pouring water over them, first over the right and then over the left hand, and in certain specified cases the ritual is repeated three times. The tradition of ritual ablutions goes back to the Pentateuch: for example, on entering the Temple and making an offering the priest had to wash his hands and feet. As early as the time of the first sanctuary there was a brass laver (Heb. *kiyor*) for ritual ablutions. This stood outside to the left of the entrance, and was later transferred to the left side of the synagogue vestibules (Ex. xxx, 17–21; 1 Kings vii, 23–40; 2 Chron. iv, 2–7). The Bezalel bowl described below may have been used for washing hands during the Seder feast, while the Warsaw set for *al maim acharonim*, mass produced by Warsaw factories of silver-plated ware, shows that this ceremony used to be widely performed.

64. Vessel for washing hands, Jerusalem, 1906–29 (cat. 88).
65. Vessels for washing hands, Warsaw, 20th cent. (cat. 89).

Wedding canopy (Heb. *huppah*) was used during the marriage ceremony. According to one interpretation the huppah symbolizes the bridegroom's home to which he leads his bride. Customarily huppahs were decorated with stars, the sources of which custom can be found in the frequently occurring biblical metaphor: "I will bless thee, and in multiplying I will multiply thy seed as the stars of the heaven..." (Gen. xv, 5, xxii, 17, xxvi, 4, xxxii, 12).

66. Canopy, Poland?, 19th cent. (cat. 90).

67. Wedding canopy, Germany?, 1891 (cat. 91).

The atarah is a decorative panel attached to the upper edge of the tallith (Yid. *tales,* or prayer shawl). The technique used in decorating the atarahs shown in this book is called "Spanish workmanship" in Yiddish. The patterns used demonstrate eastern influences which reached Poland through the Sephardic Jews who came to Lvov and Cracow during the rule of Sigismund Augustus and were brought to Zamość by Jan Zamoyski. Some of the items presented may have originated in Sasov (now in Ukraine) which was the European centre of production of such atarahs. The custom of attaching an atarah to the tallith belongs to the Ashkenazi tradition.

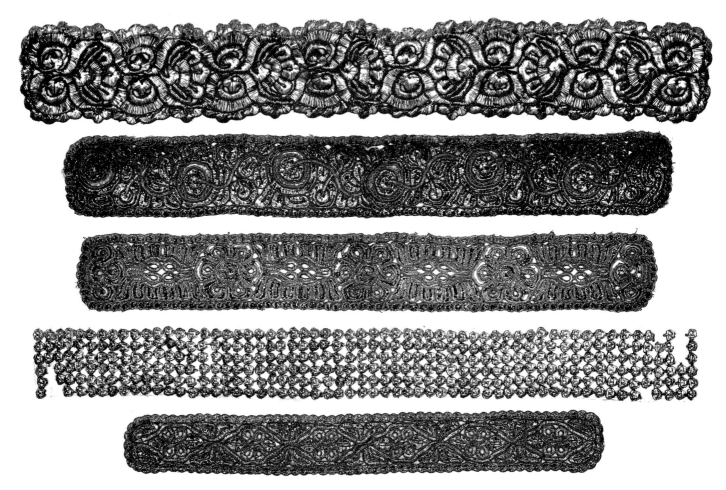

68. Atarahs, Eastern Europe, 19th cent. (from top cats. 92–96).
69. Yarmulke, Eastern Europe, 19th cent. (cat. 97)
    Walking stick, Poland, 19th cent. (cat. 98).

A yarmulke (from Turkish *Yagmurluk* or hood, in Hebrew *kipa*), also called mitska (from German *mütze*) is a small round skull-cap covering only the top of the head, which was generally worn by Jews in Central and Eastern Europe.

No biblical or talmudic rules enjoin Jews to cover their heads. The custom has its sources either in the words of the Old Testament about the high priest's attire (Ex. xxviii, 4, 36–39) or in the traditional head-dress of Babylonian scholars. It was only in the Middle Ages (13th century) that the obligation to have one's head covered at all times spread among European Jews.

At present only Orthodox Jews are obliged to always wear the yarmulke, while the Reformed Jews do not have to cover their heads, even in the synagogue.

HENRYK (HENOCH, ENRICO) GLICENSTEIN
b. Turek, 1870; d. New York, 1942.
Sculptor, painter, graphic artist.
Studied at the Academy of Fine Arts in Munich under W. von Rümann.
In 1895–1928 lived in turn in Poland, Italy and Germany; in 1928 settled in New York.
Glicenstein's main field was sculpture, initially realistic, later more expressive, showing variety in texture effects; he applied the techniques of polychromy and inlaying in his art. His mature works are static and monumental, their form compact, cubist, full of inner expression.

70. Messiah (cat. 99).

MAKS HANEMAN (HANNEMAN)
b. Łódź, 1882; d. Łódź ghetto, 1940–44

Painter. Studied at the Art College in Cracow (1907–08, 1911–14, 1918–20) under L. Wyczółkowski and T. Axentowicz; from 1916 at the Art College in Warsaw.

Haneman painted mostly landscapes of Palestine and the Tatra Mountains, genre scenes and portraits. His colours are intense and sharply contrasted. By applying paint heavily he produced a large variety of texture.

71. The Wailing Wall (cat. 100).

SZYMON BUCHBINDER

b. Radzyń Podlaski, 1853; d. Berlin, 1908 (?)

Painter. Studied under Stanisław Heyman and Adam Malinowski; in the Drawing Class in Warsaw (1869–71) under W. Gerson, R. Hadziewicz and A. Kamiński; at the Academy of Fine Arts in Vienna (1873–75) under E. von Enghert and L. Müller; in the Art College in Cracow under J. Matejko; and in the Academy of Fine Arts in Munich (1883).
In 1883 settled in Germany.
Buchbinder painted small canvases (genre and historical scenes) harking back in mood and style to the Dutch painting tradition. He depicted details of dress and accessories of the epoch with great affection.

72. Jew in Prayer (cat. 101).

NORBERT STRASSBERG b. Lvov, 1911; d. Lvov, 1941
Painter, draughtsman, graphic artist, member of Szukalski's Horned Heart Tribe.
Strassberg was inspired by literary and historic sources. He was influenced by Stanisław Szukalski and remained true to his master's fascination with the Poles' pagan past and folk art, in such painting as *Piast* and *Hutsul*. He sought subjects not only in history, but also in religion, both Judaism (*Ecstasy*, *The Day of Judgement*) and Christianity (*Christ*). He produced many portrait studies (e.g. of Bronisław Huberman), often showing figures from literature (*Golem*, *The Wandering Jew*). He had his drawings published in such satirical Lvov journals as "Szczutek" and "Wróbel na dachu".

73. Ecstasy, 1935 (cat. 102).

JÓZEF BUDKO b. Płońsk, 1888; d. Jerusalem, 1940
Graphic artist, painter.
Studied at the Drawing School in Vilna (from 1902) under I. Trutnev, and the Academy of Fine Arts in Berlin (from 1910).
Budko mainly expressed himself through graphic art, etchings and woodcuts, and his subjects are usually religious. He
produced series of prints for the *Pesach Haggadah,* the *Babylonian Talmud,* and the *Jewish Year,* the last of these presenting the
main Jewish festivals. His etchings executed in fine, precise contours and soft, winding lines reveal the influence of H. Struck
and J. Israels. In wood engravings he used contrasts of black and white and with single grooves made the contours of figures
and objects stand out from the deep, dark background. He appreciated the ornamental merits of Hebrew letters with which he
often adorned the background of his pictures.

74. Thou shalt not, 1929 (cat. 103).

ANTONI (NACHUM) ALSTER
b. Rzeszów, 1903; d. Warsaw, 1968
Graphic artist.
Self-taught artist who in 1923 studied drawing and graphic art at an evening school in Cracow.
Before the Second World War, worked as draughtsman, printer and stoker. In 1925–38, member of the Communist Party of Poland, of the Polish Workers' Party until 1948, and after 1948, of the Polish United Workers' Party. After the war, held important state positions.
Having produced his first wood engravings in the early 1920's, Alster got involved in politics and did not resume artistic work until 1963. His main works were landscapes, cityscapes, series dealing with human labour and important political events. Notable in his oeuvre are prints depicting the religious life of Jews.

75. Old Jew, 1963 (cat. 104).
76. Jews with Torah, 1965 (cat. 105).

TADEUSZ POPIEL
b. Szczucin, 1863; d. Cracow, 1913
Painter.
Studied at the Art College in Cracow (1876–81, 1881–84) under J. Matejko, W. Łuszczkiewicz, F. Cynk and L. Loeffler; and at the Academy of Fine Arts in Munich under K. von Piloty and A. Wagner.
A thorough academician, he painted religious, historical, biblical and genre subjects. His main oeuvre consists of painted decorations in churches. In 1899 he won a competition for the painted decoration for St. Stanislaus' chapel in Padua. The polychromy, completed in 1900, earned him considerable fame.

77. The Joy of the Torah (Simhath Torah) (cat. 106).
78. **Unknown painter** Rabbi with Torah (cat. 107).

ARTUR MARKOWICZ

b. Cracow, 1872; d. Cracow, 1934
Painter, draughtsman, member of the "Sztuka" (Art) Society of Polish Artists.
Studied at the Art College in Cracow (1886–95) under J. Matejko, W. Łuszczkiewicz, F. Cynk and L. Loeffler; the Academy of Fine Arts in Munich (1896–1900) under T. von Stuck; and in Paris (1900–04) under J. L. Gérôme.
Markowicz gained fame above all for his genre scenes from Jewish districts which faithfully chronicle the everyday life of Jews, from birth to death. His numerous travels (Italy, the Netherlands, Belgium, Palestine) yielded many landscape studies, the best of which are his views of Paris and the Netherlands.
His medium was pastels, more rarely oils, and he is known to have produced several prints. He was an exquisite draughtsman and a keen observer of man and nature. He favoured toned down colour schemes with the prevalence of all cool greys, blacks, intense blues and harmonious contrasts of browns and yellows.

79. Prayer (cat. 108).
80. Jews with Torah, 1933 (cat. 109).

FRYDERYK (FRYC) KLEINMAN

b. Lvov, 1897; d. Janów near Lvov, 1943
Painter, draughtsman, stage designer.
Studied in Cracow, Vienna and Paris.
Kleinman's style went through various stages: realism, German Expressionism and abstraction. Apart from painting, he also worked in graphic and stage design, and drew caricatures.

MANE KATZ (EMANUEL KATZ)
b. Krzemieńczuk (Ukraine), 1894; d. Israel, 1962
Painter, graphic artist. Studied at the Drawing School in Vilna; the Art College in Kiev; and the Académie des Beaux-Arts in Paris (1913) under M. Cormon.
In 1921 settled in Paris.
He drew his pictures freehand, applying large colour patches, and used expressive deformation and unusual textural devices. His art has been described as mystical naturalism (Ragon).
In the United States he grew interested in sculpture and produced several works in clay.
Katz was an outstanding representative of the Ecole de Paris. At first interested exclusively in Jewish subjects, he later turned to painting still-lifes, views of Paris and landscapes. Besides harmonious, monochromatic compositions, he also produced pictures in violently contrasted colour schemes under the influence of Fauvism.

81. Rabbi with Torah (cat. 110).

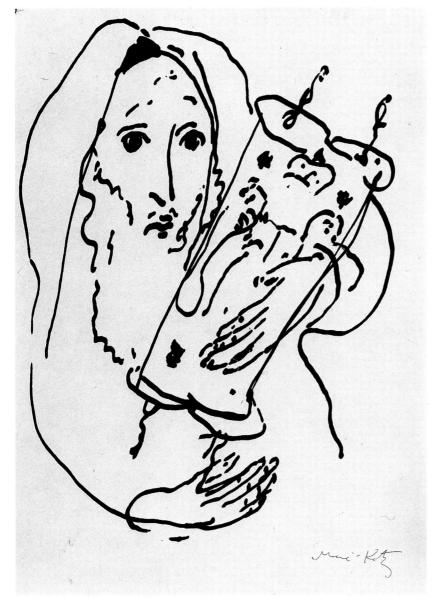

ZYGMUNT MENKES

b. Lvov, 1896; d. New York, 1986

Painter, graphic artist. Studied in the Industrial College in Lvov; at the Academy of Fine Arts in Cracow (1920–22) under W. Weiss; and in Berlin (1922) under A. Archipenko.

Menkes's paintings were composed by exploiting colour. Initially influenced by Formism (Polish Expressionism), he later tended to make his compositions flat and two-dimensional, enriching his palette and often outlining contours in black expressive lines. He exhibited in Poland, France, Germany, Austria and the United States. In New York he cooperated with the American Artists' Gallery and taught at the Art Students' League.

82. Jew with Torah (cat. 111).

WŁADYSŁAW LESZCZYŃSKI
b. Czarny Ostrów in Podolia, 1852; d. Vilna, 1916
Painter, draughtsman, author.
Studied in the Drawing Class in Warsaw (1870) under. W. Gerson; and at the Academy of Fine Arts in St. Petersburg.
Leszczyński painted realistic pictures with each detail of the composition painstakingly recreated. He produced genre and historical scenes and landscapes as well as a number of religious paintings for Vilna churches.
He wrote articles on history and his travels. As a painter, draughtsman and author he was associated with the daily and weekly press, e.g. "Tygodnik Ilustrowany", "Kurier Litewski" and "Goniec Codzienny", and for some time was the head artist of the "Biesiada Literacka". In 1913 he published and edited the satirical journal "Szubrawiec"..

83. **Artur Markowicz** Sanctification
    of the New Moon (cat. 112).
84. Jew Praying at Night, 1887 (cat. 113).

ARTUR RENNERT b. Cracow?

Painter, graphic artist. Studied at the Académie des Beaux-Arts in Paris.
Member of the Association of Jewish Painters and Sculptors in Cracow.
In 1927 settled in Paris.

85. Spice Boxes (cat. 114).
86. Sabbath, 1923 (cat. 115).

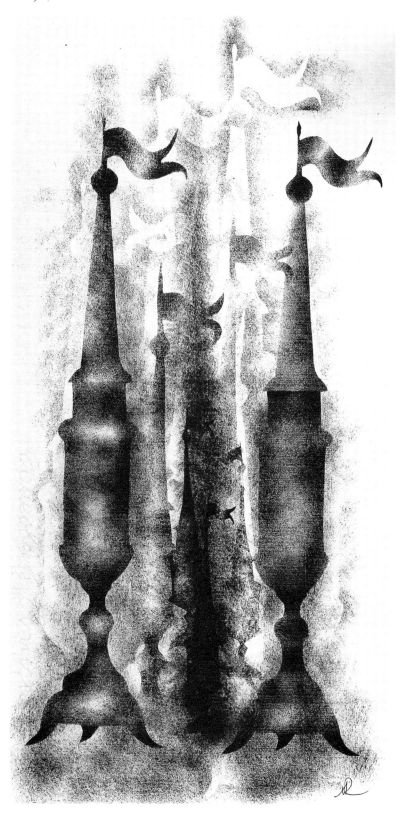

RACHELA MARCUS-SZALIT
b. Kovno (?), 1894; in 1942 deported from France to an extermination camp
Graphic artist, painter, member of the Sezession and November-gruppe.
Studied at the Academy of Fine Arts in Munich (1911–16).
Her best known and most valued works are illustrations to books by Mendele Mokher Sefarim, Shalom Aleichem, Israel
Zangwill (*The King of Schnorrers*), Martin Buber (*The Tales of the Hasidim*), Heinrich Heine, Charles Dickens, Leo Tolstoi and
Fedor Dostoyevsky.

ADOLF (ABRAHAM) MESSER
b. Sanok, 1886; d. Cracow, 1931
Painter.
Studied at the Academy of Fine Arts in Cracow (1917–18) under S. Dębicki.
Messer's realistic pictures were simple, static compositions, their colours muted and their texture smooth. He painted portrait studies and genre scenes of Jewish life.

87. Reading the Book, 1928 (cat. 116).

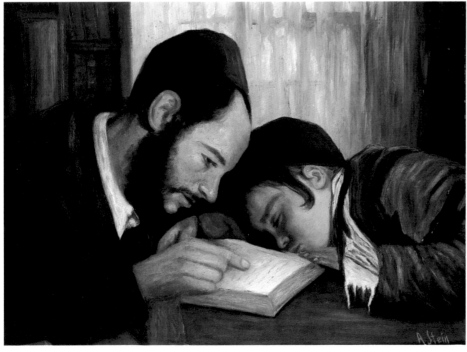

A. STEIN
Painter.
No information about his life and work.

88. Reading the Book (cat. 117).

89. **Artur Markowicz** Talmudists, 1922 (cat. 118).

MAURYCY GOTTLIEB
b. Drohobycz, 1856; d. Cracow, 1879
Painter.
Studied at the Academy of Fine Arts in Vienna (1872–74, 1877–78) under K. Meyer and K. von Blaas; the Art College in Cracow (1874–75, 1879) under J. Matejko; and the Academy of Fine Arts in Munich (1876–77) under K. von Piloty. Gottlieb was one of the first Jewish painters in Poland. He depicted scenes from the world of the Jewish Diaspora and from Polish history. In his later works Polish and Jewish themes are combined together. An important place in his oeuvre is occupied by canvases dedicated to Christ the Jew. Gottlib's talent developed in contact with the outstanding personalities of Matejko, Siemiradzki and Rodakowski, but he remained a wholly original, independent artist, in particular in portraits, which constitute the finest and most interesting part of the oeuvre of the prematurely dead artist (*Portrait of Kuranda*, 1878. *Portrait of the Artist's Sister*, *Portrait of a Jewess*). The most Matejko-like of his works is the *Head of an Old Man*, for which he used the same model who had sat for the figure of Piotr Skarga in Matejko's *Skarga's Sermon*.

90. Head of an Old Man, c. 1875
(cat. 119).

MAURYCY TRĘBACZ
b. Warsaw, 1861; died of starvation in the Łódź ghetto, 1941
Painter, draughtsman.
Studied in the Drawing Class in Warsaw (1877–80) under W. Gerson and A. Kamiński; the Art College in Cracow (1880–82) under W. Łuszczkiewicz and J. Matejko; and the Academy of Fine Arts in Munich (1882–84) under A. Wagner and F. Setz. Trębacz was one of the most popular and prolific Jewish painters of the late 19th and early 20th centuries. He painted scenes of Jewish life, "boudoir" pieces, nudes, landscapes and portraits. Initially following the academic trend, he later gave in to Impressionism, especially in his landscapes.

91. Portrait of an Old Man
    (Ben Akiba), (cat. 120).

ZYGMUNT NADEL
b. Lvov, 1854; d. Munich, 1926
Painter.
Nadel was interested first and foremost in Jewish themes and painted Polish-Jewish types in dark harmonious hues.

92. Jew in a Fur Hat Holding
    the Tallith (cat. 121).
93. Beggar (cat. 122).

WILHELM WACHTEL
b. Lvov, 1875; d. USA, 1942
Painter, graphic artist, illustrator.
Studied at the Academy of Fine Arts in Cracow (1895–89) under L. Loeffler and L. Wyczółkowski; and the Academy of Fine Arts in Munich.
Wachtel painted mostly portraits and nostalgic compositions of Jewish small-town life. Some of his works (especially his pastels) are rendered with precision and faithfulness to detail; in others he moved from a painstaking reproduction of reality to free composition, using broad brushstrokes.

94. Study of a Jewish Boy, 1916 (cat. 123).

MAKSYMILIAN ELJOWICZ, b. Raciąż near Płock, 1890; d. Treblinka, 1942
Painter, graphic artist.
Studied at the Art College in Warsaw (1911, 1920).
Eljowicz painted realistic portraits in a traditional style, but was much better as a graphic designer; he employed simplified cubist forms and flat, geometric surfaces outlined in clear linear contours (*Rabbi*).
During the Second World War, together with Józef Śliwniak, he produced stained-glass windows for the reception room of the Jewish Community Hall and the murals *Job* and *Working Jews*.

95. Rabbi (cat. 124).

ANTONI GRABARZ JARZYMSKI
b. Warsaw, 1904; d. Bydgoszcz, 1965
Painter, draughtsman, interior designer.
Studied at the Art College in Warsaw (1922–28) under T. Pruszkowski; and in Paris (1936).
Grabarz produced portraits, genre scenes, murals, caricatures and interior designs.
Initially rendered realistically, almost naturalistically, in time his subjects, mostly women, tended to become idealized. After the war, he came under the influence of Post-Impressionism and Cubism.

96. Jewish Furrier, 1937
   (cat. 125).

SAMUEL HIRSZENBERG
b. Łódź (Drohobycz), 1865; d. Jerusalem, 1908
Painter.
Studied at the Crafts School in Łódź; the Art College in Cracow (1881–83) under F. Szynalewski, I. Jabłoński and
W. Łuszczkiewicz; the Academy of Fine Arts in Munich (1883) under A. Wagner; and the Académie Colarossi in Paris (1889).
In 1907, appointed director of the Bezalel School of Crafts in Jerusalem.
Hirszenberg was a prolific painter, highly appreciated and popular during his lifetime. His oeuvre is diversified and includes
monumental realistic compositions based on literary themes (often on Jewish subjects), genre scenes and portraits, as well as
landscapes where he successfully exploited impressionist techniques.
Hirszenberg also produced decorative panneaux for palatial residences in Munich and for the Poznański mansion in Łódź.

97. Jew with a Walking Stick, 1902 (cat. 126).

LEON LEWKOWICZ
b. Rawa, 1890 (1888); d. Chimkent (USSR), 1950
Painter.
Studied at the Academy of Fine Arts in Cracow (1913–20) under T. Axentowicz.
Lewkowicz painted sentimental portraits of children and young women, expressive portraits of old men, genre scenes and few landscapes.

98. Head of an Old Man, 1921 (cat. 127).
99. **Artur Markowicz** Jew at Work (cat. 128).
100. Jew at Work (cat. 129).

MOJŻESZ (MAURYCY) RYNECKI b. Warsaw, 1885; d. Warsaw, 1942
Painter, draughtsman. Studied at the Art College in Warsaw (1904–07).
Rynecki painted mainly genre scenes of Jewish life, in particular craftsmen at work – smiths, shoemakers, tailors, carpenters – as well as religious pictures: *Jews Reading the Book, Maggid,* or *Prayer on the Day of Atonement.*

JOACHIM KAHANE

b. Ząbki near Tarnopol, 1890; d. Łódź, 1943 (?)

Metalwork artist, teacher of drawing in the Hebrew College in Łódź.

No information on the course of his studies.

Kahane created portraits, landscapes and still-lifes. His portraits are strikingly penetrating psychological studies of the sitters, characterized by faithfulness to detail and fine linear contours. He often tackled Jewish themes (*Jew with Etrog, Seder*). Kahane also produced liturgical objects, such as hanukkah lamps, Torah shields and Seder plates.

101. Head of a Jew, 1936 (cat. 130).
102. Monk, 1931 (cat. 131).

ARTUR SZYK

b. Łódź, 1894; d. New York, 1951

Painter, illustrator, caricaturist.

Studied at the Ecole des Beaux-Arts (from 1908) and the Académie Julian in Paris; and the Academy of Fine Arts in Cracow (from 1913) under T. Axentowicz.

Szyk gained fame above all as a miniature painter. In his works – most frequently illustrations in the form of vignettes and initials which together with the text constituted a decorative whole – he reverted to the style and technique of mediaeval French and eastern miniatures.

The Kalisz Statutes – 45 plates of illustrated text of privileges, known as the Kalisz Statutes, which Prince Boleslaus the Tall granted the Jews in 1264. The miniatures refer directly to the individual articles of the statute or else show events from the history of Jews in Poland. The text is in nine languages: Latin, Polish, Hebrew, Yiddish, French, English, German, Italian and Spanish.

103. The Kalisz Statute, miniature no. 19, 1926-30 (cat. 132).
104. The Kalisz Statute, miniature no. 5, 1927 (cat. 133).

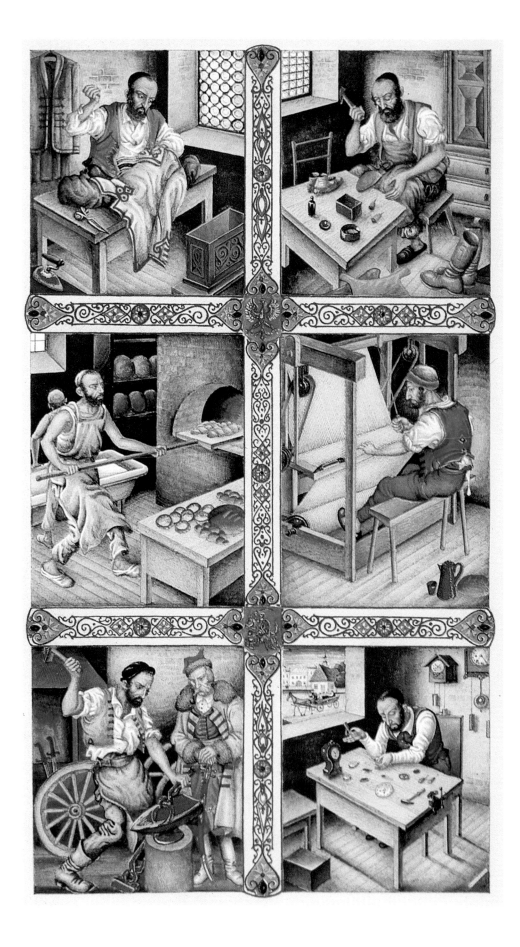

MOJŻESZ LEJBOWSKI
b. Nowogródek, 1876; d. Vilna, 1942/43
Painter, journalist.
Studied at the Académie des Beaux-Arts in Paris (1899–1900, 1904) under M. Bonnet.
Lejbowski was a talented draughtsman who also painted in oil. He was interested in portraiture and landscape, especially small, intimate views of Vilna.

105. Courtyard in Vilna (cat. 134).
106. Old Synagogue in Vilna, 1928 (cat. 135).

RAFAŁ LEWIN
Painter.
No information about his life and
work.

RAFAŁ (RAFAEL) CHWOLES
b. Vilna, 1913
Painter, graphic artist.
Studied at the Fine Arts Department of the Stephen Báthory University in Vilna with A. Sturman and M. Kulesza.
Came to Poland in 1959 and settled in Paris in 1969.
Initially Chwoles created melancholy compositions, mostly on the subject of Vilna, his native town. After the war, in a series of paintings, mostly gouaches, he tackled the theme of Jewish martyrdom, a subject to which he also returned in later years. An important element in his oeuvre is his multi-coloured, expressive cycle of pictures composed of matching colour patches, frequently in dark contours.
In 1962 he exhibited in Warsaw oils from the series the *Holocaust*.

108. Tailors' Synagogue in Vilna, 1962 (cat. 137).

107. Jewish Suburb in Vilna (Łukiszki), 1962 (cat. 136).

ADOLF BEHRMAN (BEHRMANN)
b. Riga, 1876 (1880); d. Białystok ghetto, 1942
Painter, member of the "Silver Cart" group.
Studied at the Academy of Fine Arts in Munich (1900–04) and in Paris.
Behrman painted mainly genre scenes and landscapes, as well as sketches from his artistic trips to Palestine, Egypt, Tunisia
and Morocco. In his paintings the major element is colour; the violently contrasted hues are applied in free, rapid brushstrokes.

109. Jewish Water Carrier in the Market
Place in Kazimierz Dolny (cat. 138).

SYMCHE BINEM (SIMON) TRACHTER
b. Lublin, 1890 (1894); d. Treblinka, 1942
Painter.
Studied at the Art College in Warsaw (1911) with S. Lentz; the Academy of Fine Arts in Cracow (1916–20) with J. Mal-
czewski and S. Dębicki; and in Vienna and Paris.
Member of the Association of Jewish Painters and Sculptors in Cracow.
Trachter painted mainly oil landscapes and still-lifes and was also interested in drawing. He composed his pictures by means of
harmonious hues laid on in small patches of colour, and often used linear contours.

110. **Maurycy Trębacz** Street
in Kazimierz on the Vistula
(cat. 139).
111. Landscape (Kazimierz Dolny),
1929 (cat. 140).

EFRAIM AND MENASZE SEIDENBEUTEL

b. Warsaw, 1903; murdered in the concentration camp of Flossenburg in April 1943

Painters, members of the "Szkoła Warszawska" group and "Blok" Union of Polish Artists.

Studied at the Art College in Warsaw under T. Pruszkowski and W. Skoczylas.

The Seidenbeutels often worked together and their individual pieces are hard to distinguish. They painted still-lifes, landscapes, portraits and occasionally figural compositions executed in pastel, whitened tones (e.g. *Girl with a Dove in a Cage*). They treated the subject merely as a pretext for depicting the play of light and colour: in their still-lifes they applied harmonious, original contrast of tone, and in landscapes tried to capture the changes of light and convey the wealth of colours and hues in nature.

112. View of Kazimierz on the Vistula (cat. 141).

113. Small Town, 1928 (cat. 142).

MARCIN KITZ b. Lvov, 1891 (1894); d. Lvov, 1943
Painter, graphic artist. Studied at the Technical University in Lvov and at the same time painting with A. Rajchman
and S. Batowski; at the Academy of Fine Arts in Cracow (1919–20) under I. Pieńkowski; the Ludwika Mehofferowa Free
School of Painting and Drawing; and in Berlin, Munich and Vienna.
Kitz painted most frequently genre scenes and landscapes, more rarely still-lifes and portraits. His light, luminous colour
schemes and fragmentary "randomly selected" views are directly related to impressionist painting.

114. **Unknown painter** Typical Characters from Kazimierz on the Vistula (cat. 143).

115. Water Carrier (cat. 144).

JÓZEF BADOWER
b. Tomaszów Mazowiecki, c. 1900; d. 1939–45 (?)
Painter, member of the "Independents" group.
Studied at the Academy of Fine Arts in Cracow (?).
Badower painted portraits, landscapes and still-lifes, was the author of frescoes in the synagogue in Sosnowiec and designed
stage scenery for the municipal theatre in the same city.

VINCENT (ICCHAK) BRAUNER

b. Łódź, 1887; d. Auschwitz, 1944

Painter, graphic artist, metalwork artist, stage designer, member of the Yung Yiddish group.

Studied in J. Kacenbogen's private school in Łódź; attended violin classes at the Berlin Conservatoire (1908–12), at the same time studying at the Hofschule für die bildenden Künste.

Brauner's early works, rendered in light, sunny hues, display post-impressionist influences. Later expressionist elements – deformation, colour dissonance – appeared. In the 1930's, he mainly produced artistic metalwork.

He was influenced by Marc Chagall and Jankiel Adler. He also worked for the theatre. In 1921, he designed expressionistic sets for Ansky's *The Dybbuk*, staged by D. Herman in the Jewish theatre in Łódź. Together with the poet M. Broderson and the composer H. Kohn. Brauner formed a puppet-theatre called "Chad-Gajdon", for which he carved some thirty marionettes.

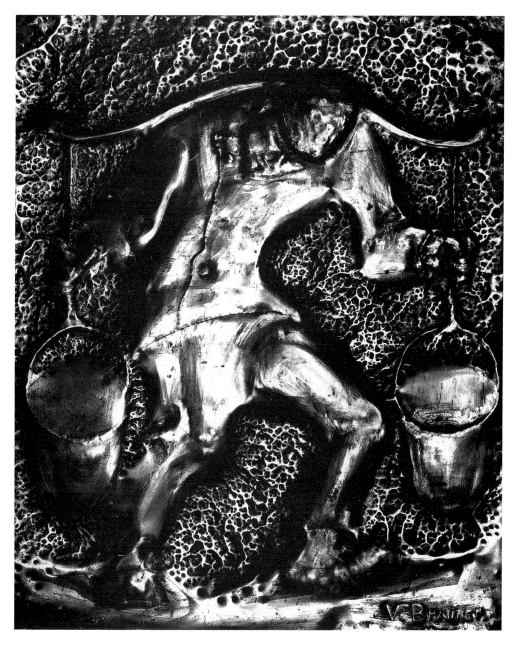

116. Water Carrier (cat. 145).

MAREK SZWARC
b. Zgierz, 1892; d. Paris, 1958
Sculptor, metalwork artist, painter, graphic artist, member of the Yung Yiddish group.
Studied at the Académie des Beaux-Arts in Paris (1910–13) under A. Mercié; and the Academy of Fine Arts in Cracow (1918–19) under K. Laszczka.
Initially Szwarc engaged himself in sculpture, drawing, graphic art and painting. He produced landscapes, portraits, genre scenes and religious and symbolical compositions. Later he switched to artistic metalwork mainly in copper. His earlier, stylized compositions, consisting of decorative arrangements of lines and planes, gradually evolved towards synthetic forms drawing on ancient and primitive art and naturalism.

117. Shepherd with a Lamb (cat. 146).

ERNÖ ERB
b. Lvov (?), 1878 (1890); d. Janów camp in Lvov, 1943
Self-taught painter.
Erb painted still-lifes, landscapes, cityscapes and genre scenes. His paintings, with their synthetic forms and rough texture, are rendered in light hues.

118. At the Market (cat. 147).

DAWID (DANIEL) GREIFENBERG (GRAJFENBERG) b. Warsaw, 1909; d. Treblinka, 1942
Painter, member of the "Blok" Union of Polish Artists. Studied in the Art College in Warsaw (1927–32) under M. Kotarbiński. In the Warsaw ghetto, Greifenberg taught in the School of Applied Graphic Design and Technical Drawing. He painted portraits, still-lifes and landscapes in violent colours laid on with free, rapid brushstrokes.

119. Stream (cat. 148).
120. Small Town
(cat. 149).

NATAN KORZEŃ b. Płock, 1895; d. Vilna, 1941
Painter, stage designer.
Studied at the Art College in Warsaw under S. Lentz and T. Pruszkowski.
Korzeń's style has its roots in Impressionism and is described by critics as colouristic-textural. Rendered in broad brushstrokes, his works demonstrate the artist's great feeling for colour and light.

121. Cottages (cat. 150).

HENRYK (HERSZ) RABINOWICZ
b. Warsaw, c. 1900; d. Treblinka, 1942
Painter, graphic artist.
No information on the course of his studies.
Rabinowicz painted mostly oil landscapes and still-lifes, rendered in free brushstrokes in light, luminous hues.

122. Ruins of a House (cat. 151).

SAMUEL FINKELSTEIN
b. Sandomierz (Łódź), 1890 (1889, 1892, 1895); d. Treblinka, 1942 (?)
Painter, member of the "Unicorn" and "Start" groups.
Studied at the Academy of Fine Arts in Cracow (1913–14) under W. Weiss; and in Vienna.
Finkelstein painted portraits, figural scenes, landscapes and still-lifes. He freely applied large splashes of colour and introduced slightly misshapen and simplified forms.

123. Houses by the Water, 1930 (cat. 152).

HENRYK LEWENSZTADT

b. 1893

Painter.

Studied at the Art College in Warsaw (from 1911); and in Munich.

In the early stage, Lewensztadt worked in pastels in harmonious colour schemes and oils in strong, contrasted, darkened tones. His forms were misshapen and his subjects depicted in a pointedly expressive way.

124. Zakopane (cat. 153).

ABRAHAM NEUMANN
b. Sierpc, 1873; d. Cracow, 1943
Painter, graphic artist, member of the "Sztuka" Society of Polish Artists.
Studied at the Academy of Fine Arts in Cracow (1897–1902) under J. Malczewski and L. Wyczółkowski; and the Académie Julian in Paris (1900).
Neumann painted mountain and forest views, spring thaws and summer sunsets, townscapes (Kazimierz on the Vistula, Kalwaria Zebrzydowska), and in the 1920's he also produced figural compositions, portraits and still-lifes.
He travelled a lot, visiting England, Belgium, the Netherlands, Germany and the United States. In 1904 and 1926–27 he was in Palestine (*Jeruzalem*, *Street in Safed*, *Arab Village*).

127. Kalwaria Zebrzydowska, 1917 (cat. 156).

125. **Samuel Hirszenberg** Rural Landscape in Winter (cat. 154).
126. **Artur Markowicz** Brügge: Street in Sunlight, 1920 (cat. 155).

LEON ROZENBLUM (ROSENBLUM)
b. Cracow, 1883; d. Auschwitz, 1942 (1943)
Painter.
Studied at the Academy of Fine Arts in Cracow (1898–1905) under F. Cynk, J. Stanisławski and L. Wyczółkowski.
Rozenblum painted mostly landscapes, often minor, seemingly randomly chosen pieces of scenery. He composed them using large harmonious patches of colour, occasionally inspired by the impressionist tradition.

128. Winter Landscape (cat. 157).

NATAN SZPIGEL (SPIGEL)
b. Łódź, 1890; d. ?, 1943
Painter, draughtsman, member of the "Silver Cart" and "Start" groups.
Studied in Łódź, Dresden (1923–25) and Paris.
Szpigel's art was influenced by the impressionist tradition of the Yung Yiddish and Bunt groups. He tackled social and religious subjects, painted portraits, landscapes and still-lifes.
During the Second World War, he produced many drawings depicting everyday life in the Łódź ghetto.

129. Before the Cottage (cat. 158).

HENRYK CYTRYN
b. Opatów, 1911; d. Białystok, 1941 (1943)
Painter, graphic artist.
Studied at the Academy of Fine Arts in Warsaw (until 1931).
Cytryn painted landscapes, genre scenes, portraits and still-lifes in which colour played a paramount role.

130. Boy with a Cart, 1939 (cat. 159).

HENRYK GOTLIB
b. Cracow, 1890; d. South Godstone (Britain), 1966

Painter, graphic artist, sculptor, stage designer, journalist, art critic; member of the following groups: Formists, "Awan-garda", "Group of Ten", "New Generation", "Zwornik", the "Cercle des Artistes Polonais", and the London Group.

Studied at the Academy of Fine Arts in Cracow (1908–10) under J. Unierzyński and W. Weiss; the Law and Economics Faculty of the Jagiellonian University in Cracow; the Kunstgewerbeschule (1910–13) and the Law Faculty of the University in Vienna; and the Academy of Fine Arts in Munich (1913) under Angelo Jank.

Lived in France in 1923–29, subsequently returned to Poland and in 1939 settled in Britain.

Initially Gotlib was a formist (expressionist). Following a period of experimentation he became one of the leading representatives of colourism in Polish painting. His drawing was sketchy and his palette light and luminous. After the war his paintings became more ascetic, with a preponderance of dark hues and rough texture.

131. Breton Landscape: On the Seashore, 1929? (cat. 160).

EMIL SCHINAGEL (SZINAGEL, SINAGEL)
b. Drohojów, 1899; d. Lvov, 1943
Doctor of medicine, painter, graphic artist, illustrator, journalist; member of the "Zwornik" group and the Association of
(Jewish Painters and Sculptors in Cracow.
Studied at the Academy of Fine Arts in Cracow (1919) under T. Axentowicz; and in the Academy of Fine Arts in Brussels
(1930) under van Haalen.
Schinagel's media were oils, frescoes and graphic design. His palette ranged from toned down compositions to expressive
colour contrasts. He painted with considerable facility and applied a specific deformation and flattening of form.

132. Pension (cat. 161).

133. In the Cab (cat. 162).

134. **Adolf Behrman** Eastern Landscape, 1933 (cat. 163).
135. Apiary (Bee-hives), 1931 (cat. 164).

GIZELA HUFNAGLÓWNA-KLIMASZEWSKA-ARCTOWA b. Warsaw, 1903
Painter, member of "Ars Feminae", "Kolor", "Blok" Union of Polish Artists and "Powiśle". Studied at the Art College in Warsaw (1924–30) under T. Pruszkowski, S. Noakowski and W. Jastrzębowski, graduated in 1949.
Her favourite genre is landscape. In her enchantingly lyrical, melancholy views, colour and light play the most prominent role.

BERTA (BIMA) GRÜNBERG
b. Gródek Jagielloński, 1909; lives in France
Painter, member of the "Grupa Krakowska".
Studied at the Academy of Fine Arts in Cracow (1931–34) under W. Jarocki.
In 1937 settled in France.
While she was still a member of the "Grupa Krakowska", Grünberg painted mainly still-lifes and landscapes rendered in expressive patches of colour laid on in free strokes, sometimes almost in a divisionist fashion; her forms tend towards simplification and geometrization.

136. Landscape (cat. 165).
137. Landscape with Houses (cat. 166).

SASZA (SZAJE) BLONDER (ANDRÉ BLONDEL)
b. Czortków, 1909; d. Paris, 1949
Painter. Member of the "Żywi" (Alive) group, "Grupa Krakowska" and "Artistes Méridionaux" in Toulouse.
Studied in Paris (from 1926 and in 1929), including architecture at the Ecole Nationale Supérieur des Beaux-Arts; and the
Academy of Fine Arts in Cracow (1931–34) with T. Axentowicz, W. Jarocki and F. Pautsch.
In 1937 he settled in France.
Initially inspired by Chagall, Modigliani and Soutine, later he tended increasingly towards abstraction. While still a member of
the "Grupa Krakowska", he took up the subject of imprisonment, political demonstrations and street riots which he rendered
in strongly geometrical two dimensional forms. In time he turned to abstract compositions in expressive bright hues.
In 1945 he started using bright, determined colour schemes, but preserving his old method of building a picture of
interlinking, schematic forms. In this period he favoured landscape, still-lifes and flowers.

ANIELA CUKIERÓWNA
b. Warsaw, 1900; d. Warsaw, 1944
Graphic artist, draughtswoman.
Studied in K. Krzyżanowski's studio; and the Art College in Warsaw (from 1923) under T. Pruszkowski, M. Kotarbiński,
W. Jastrzębowski and E. Czerwiński.
Her favourite genre was cityscape, and she produced series depicting various towns: *Warsaw Views, Gardens,* and *Picturesque
Towns.* She also designed stained-glass windows and worked as a journalist.
Not many of her works have survived. Some perished during the war, and some were destroyed by the artist who was
extremely demanding and critical towards her own work.

ADAM (ABRAHAM) HERSZAFT
b. Warsaw, 1886; d. Treblinka, 1942
Graphic artist, painter, author, art critic.
Studied at the Art College in Warsaw (from 1904); the Académie des Beaux-Arts in Paris (1907–11); in Munich and Italy.
First and foremost Herszaft was a graphic artist. His profoundly lyrical compositions are executed in soft lines, their drawing free and accurate, with skilfully managed chiaroscuro effects. He was mostly interested in landscape (the series *Old Berlin*, portfolios of views of Venice and Sicily) and portrait (series of idealized female likenesses).

139. Sicily (cat. 168).

138. View of St. Casimir's Convent from Okólnik Street, 1933 (cat. 167).

FISZEL ZYLBERBERG (ZBER)

b. Płock, 1909; d. Auschwitz, 1942

Graphic artist, painter, member of the "Black and White" group and the "Blok" Union of Polish Artists.

Studied at the Academy of Fine Arts in Warsaw (1928–33) as an extramural student under W. Skoczylas, L. Wyczółkowski, M. Kotarbiński and F. S. Kowarski.

Zylberberg is known mainly as a graphic artist, but he also worked as a painter. His wood engravings, although as a rule restricted to black and white, are of a high artistic standard due to their chiaroscuro effects, sharp contrasts and free drawing.

140. Cello Player, 1934
(cat. 169).

MOSZE BERNSTEIN
b. Bereza Kartuska, 1920
Painter, graphic artist.
Studied in Vilna (until 1939).
Until 1947 lived in the Soviet Union, in 1948 settled in Israel.
Bernstein uses various media: oil, pastel, watercolour, pen and ink. The major part of his oeuvre consists of black and white paintings, and the main theme of his nostalgic, lyrical works are views of Jewish towns.

141. Klezmer, 1982 (cat. 170).

FELIKS FRYDMAN b. Warsaw, 1897; d. Warsaw, 1942
Painter, graphic artist, art critic.
Studied in Warsaw and Paris.
In the 1930's, president of the Association of Jewish Artists. In the Warsaw ghetto during the Second World War, member of the Cultural Council of the Judenrat.
Frydman painted portraits, genre scenes, still-lifes and landscapes. His works are characterized by free drawing, broad, rapid brushstrokes and pure, soft colours.

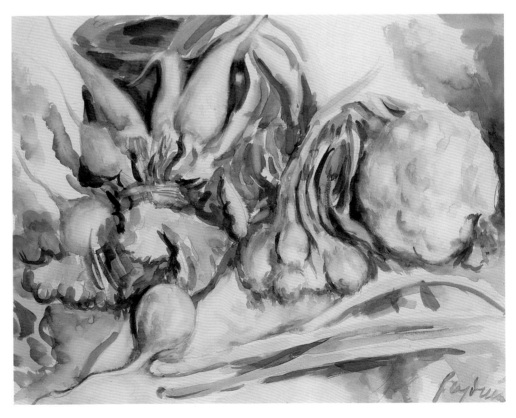

ELIASZ KANAREK
b. Warsaw, 1901; d. USA, 1972
Painter, graphic artist, member of the St. Luke Fraternity and the "Blok" Union of Polish Artists.
Studied at the Art College in Warsaw (from 1923) under T. Pruszkowski.
In 1939 settled in the United States.
Kanarek's oeuvre is not particularly well known since not many of his pre-war works have come down to us. He painted religious pictures (*St. Theresa, St. Francis of Assisi*) and portraits, more rarely landscapes and flower and figural compositions.

145. Idyll, c. 1931 (cat. 174).
146. **Efraim and Menasze Seidenbeutel**
Girl with a Pigeon in a Cage (cat. 175).

HENRYK BERLEWI
b. Warsaw, 1894, d. Paris, 1967
Painter, art critic, member of the "Blok" group.
Studied at the Art College in Warsaw (1904–09) while still a secondary school pupil; at the Academy of Fine Arts in
Antwerp (1909–10) under J. Varendt; the Ecole des Beaux-Arts in Paris (1911–12) under P. Maurou; and the School of
Drawing in Warsaw under J. Kauzik.
Berlewi's early pictures were in the style of Jewish Expressionism inspired by Chagall's art. When he was in Berlin in 1922–23
he came under the influence of Constructivism. In 1923, at the Gross Berliner Kunst Austellung, in the section Novem-
bergruppe he showed his first work composed according to the principles of mechano-facture. Back in Poland he joined
the Blok group of artists and became one of the leading exponents of Polish Constructivism. He propounded his own
theory of "mechano-facture" which he published in a booklet in Warsaw in 1924.

147. Chonon and Leah, poster to
Dybbuk, 1921 (cat. 176).

148. **Zygmunt Menkes**
By the Well (Biblical Scene), 1923
(cat. 177).

HUGO STEINER-PRAG

b. Prague, 1880; d. New York, 1945

Graphic artist, painter, stage designer.

Studied in Prague. In 1907–33 taught at the Municipal Academy in Leipzig, dismissed when Hitler came to power. Left for Prague where he established a school of applied art. In 1939 emigrated to the United States.

Steiner worked almost exclusively in book design, including covers, jackets and graphic layout. He provided illustrations, for example, for *Mahzor* (1936) and Gustav Meyrink's *Der Golem*.

149. Golem, from the series *The Golem: A Prague Fantasy*, 1916 (cat. 178).

150. Alchemists' Street (Golden Street), from the series *The Golem: A Prague Fantasy*, 1916 (cat. 179).

BRUNO SCHULZ

b. Drohobycz, 1892; d. Drohobycz, 1942

Author, painter, draughtsman, graphic artist.

Studied architecture at the Technical University in Lvov (until 1913); and the Academy of Fine Arts in Vienna (1914).
Schulz produced drawings (in pencil and pen and ink) and graphic prints (cliché verre), some of them illustrations to his own
stories. In 1920–22, he worked on a series of prints entitled *The Booke of Idolatry* modelled on numerous earlier drawings similar
in style and subject matter. Schulz's is a specific kind of realism employing deformation and caricature-like exaggeration.

151. Self-portrait with Stanisław Weingarten, 1921 (cat. 180).

152. Sadistic women, 1919 (cat. 181).

153. **Bruno Schulz** Grotesque: Barrel Organ Player in the Courtyard, 1936 (cat. 182).

154. **Bruno Schulz** By the Sick Bed, 1926 (cat. 183).

JAN GOTARD
b. Warsaw, 1898; d. 1943
Painter, graphic artist, member of the St. Luke Fraternity and the "Blok" Union of Polish Artists.
Studied in K. Krzyżanowski's private school of drawing (1914); law at Warsaw University; at the Art College in Warsaw (1923–27) under T. Pruszkowski and W. Skoczylas. In 1929–37, assistant of T. Pruszkowski in the Warsaw Academy of Fine Arts.
Gotard's oeuvre includes above all portraits and characteristic portrait studies, but he also painted landscapes, still-lifes and nudes. In his early works we may discern influences of 15th and 16th century Dutch painting as well as of the Italian Caravaggionists. The characteristic features of his paintings are dark, almost monochromatic colour schemes, meticulous drawing, smooth and luminous brushwork. In the 1930's the artist toned down the sharpness of contours and contrasts of light and shade and made his palette lighter and his figures, softly emerging from the background, became illusory and ethereal. The painting that reveals best the strange, grotesque atmosphere of Gotard's work is his *Fairy-tale about Cinderella*, 1937.

155. Fairy-tale about Cinderella, 1937 (cat. 184).

156. **Jan Gotard** Girl in a White Hat (cat. 186).

157. **Jan Gotard** Fortune-teller, 1933 (cat. 185).

RAJMUND KANELBA (KANELBAUM)
b. Warsaw, 1897; d. London, 1966
Painter, member of the "New Generation" group.
Studied at the Art College in Warsaw (from 1916) under S. Lentz and T. Pruszkowski; the Academy of Fine Arts in Vienna; and in Paris.
In 1926 settled in Paris and in 1956–59 lived in turn in Paris, London and New York.
Kanelba painted portraits, flowers, views of streets and figural scenes. His early works are characterized by a correct style of drawing and a tendency towards idealization. Later, under the influence of the Ecole de Paris, his forms lost their angularity and severity, colours became harmoniously toned down and interesting effects of texture are noticeable.

158. **Henryk Gotlib** Study of a Woman Wearing a Hat, 1923 (cat. 187).   159. Female Study (cat. 188).

NATAN ALTMAN
b. ?; d. Łódź, 1929
Painter.
Altman painted landscapes, still-lifes and portraits which demonstrate a penetrating characterization of the sitter, precision and attentiveness to detail. His portraits of Mr. and Mrs. Brown are particulary interesting.

LEOPOLD HOROWITZ

b. Rozgony near Kosice, 1839; d. Vienna, 1917
Painter.
Studied in Kosice under V. Klimkovic; and at the Academy of Fine Arts in Vienna (1853–59) under K. von Blaas, P. I. N. Geiger, K. Meyer and K. Wurzinger.
Horowitz was a well-known portraitist, especially popular with the rich middle class and aristocracy. He also painted genre scenes on Jewish themes and historical canvases (*Anniversary of the Destruction of the Temple in Jerusalem,* 1870).
The popularity he enjoyed often had an adverse effect on the quality of his work. He painted hastily, often from photographs, according to a certain pattern. A dark, toned down palette, thinly, meticulously applied paint – these are the main features of Horowitz's style. However in his best works he succeeded in steering clear of schematic composition and colour schemes, and then his expressive portraits showed not only beautiful costumes, but also the character of the sitter.

160. Portrait of a Woman (Mrs. Braun), 1900 (cat. 189).
161. Portrait of Helena Hermanówna, 1881 (cat. 190).

LEOPOLD GOTTLIEB

b. Drohobycz, 1883 (1879); d. Paris, 1934

Painter, draughtsman, member of the Group of Five, the Hagebund of Vienna and the "Rytm" Association of Polish Artists. Studied at the Academy of Fine Arts in Cracow (1896–1902) under J. Malczewski and T. Axentowicz; and the Academy of Fine Arts in Munich (1902–04) under A. Ažbé.

In his early oeuvre, mostly portraits, Gottlieb used deformation enhanced by sharply outlined contours. After the First World War he turned to scenes of human labour and dynamic religious compositions, making their colours sharp and vivid and their forms angular. Towards the late 1920's his pictures acquired a calm static composition and were executed almost exclusively in various shades of white.

162. Portrait of Dr Ber
     Kupczyk, c. 1907 (cat. 191).

JERZY (GEORG) MERKEL
b. Lvov, 1881; d. Vienna, 1976
Painter, member of the Hagebund and Sezession of Vienna.
Studied at the Academy of Fine Arts in Cracow (1903–07) under J. Mehoffer and S. Wyspiański; and in Paris (1905–08, 1909–14).
As a student in Cracow Merkel came under the influence of Stanisław Wyspiański, as can be seen, for example, in his *Portrait of a Man*. Later, in Paris, he evolved his own style: his paintings became geometrical, linear, flat, and muted in colour.
Merkel's is a specific, personal kind of classicism, revealed not only in themes. The calm, static mood and quiescence of his canvases turn the depicted human forms into dream figures. Although small in size, his works are conceived and executed as monumental compositions.

163. Portrait of a Man, 1906 (cat. 192).

ROMAN KRAMSZTYK
b. Warsaw, 1885; d. Warsaw, 1942

Painter, draughtsman, member of the Group of Five, one of the founders of the "Rytm" Association of Polish Artists. Studied at the Academy of Fine Arts in Cracow (1903–04) with J. Mehoffer; and in A. E. Herstein's studio in Warsaw. Kramsztyk's oeuvre consists mainly of portraits, landscapes and still-lifes. In his earlier works, executed in dark colour schemes, sharply outlined contours break up compact solid masses. Towards the end of the 1920's his palette became lighter and softer, and half-tones began to appear; his drawing tended to be more precise.

The outbreak of the second world war found Kramsztyk in Warsaw. An inmate of the Warsaw ghetto, he was killed by the Nazis during the so-called Grossaktion on 6 August 1942. The Ringelblum Archives include Kramsztyk's sanguine drawing showing a Jewish family in the ghetto.

164. Portrait of a Man 1928 (cat. 194).
165. Man in a Bowler Hat (cat. 193).

IZRAEL LEJZEROWICZ

b. Łódź, 1900 (1902); d. Auschwitz, 1944

Painter, graphic artist, art critic, member of the "Start" group.

Studied in Rome and perhaps at the Academy of Fine Arts in Berlin, though this has never been confirmed.

First and foremost Lejzerowicz was a portraitist. The composition of his portraits is calm and static, and his colour schemes are dark and toned down. During the Second World War, in the Łódź ghetto, he painted portraits of Chaim Rumkowski (president of the Jewish Council), scenes of everyday life (*Women Peeling Vegetables*) and cityscapes (*Bridge in the Łódź Ghetto*).

166. Portrait of a Man, 1930 (cat. 195).
167. Portrait of an Old Woman, 1941 (cat. 196).
168. **Samuel Finkelstein** Self-portrait (cat. 197).

STANISŁAWA CENTNERSZWEROWA

b. Warsaw, 1889; d. Białystok ghetto, 1942

Painter, member of the "Muse" association. Studied in A. E. Herstein's studio in Warsaw, and in Paris under H. J. G. Martin and E. Renard.

Centnerszwerowa was associated with the artists from the Yung Ydish group. Initially influenced by Formism, or Polish Expressionism, she later turned to post-Impressionism.

EMIL ORLIK
b. Prague, 1870; d. Berlin, 1932
Graphic artist, painter.
Studied in Munich under I. L. Raab, H. Knirr and W. Linden-Schmitt.
Orlik was above all a graphic designer, skilled in intaglio techniques, wood engraving and lithography.
His extremely painterly style in his early compositions gradually evolved towards an exaggerated, simplified line for which he was indebted to Japanese woodcut. A major part of his oeuvre consists of portraits.
He produced a series of likenesses of outstanding individuals (Bach, Michelangelo) in which he sometimes imitated old graphic forms, and a number of portraits of his contemporaries. Towards the end of his life he often reverted to a method by which the head was painstakingly recreated while the rest of the figure, costume and backgound were treated sketchily (Gustav Mahler, Richard Strauss, Ernst Haeckel, a German painter settled in Munich).

169. Ernst Haeckel, 1901 (cat. 198).

MAX LIEBERMANN
b. Berlin, 1847; d. Berlin, 1935
Painter, graphic artist, draughtsman, one of the founders of the Berlin Sezession.
Studied in K. Steffeck's private school (1866–68); and the Grossherzliche Kunstschule in Weimar (1869–71) under F. Pauwels and F. Thumann.
In his early career, Liebermann was interested first and foremost in social subjects and executed realistic scenes from the life of workers, peasants and craftsmen. Later he began to work in the impressionist manner and painted landscapes, genre scenes, religious themes, portraits and self-portraits.

170. Portrait of Hermann Cohen
     (cat. 199).

LEON BAKST (LEW ROSENBERG)
b. Grodno, 1866; d. Paris, 1924
Painter, graphic artist, stage designer, illustrator, one of the founders of the "Mir Isskustva" group.
Studied at the Art Academy in St. Petersburg and the Académie Julian in Paris.
In his early career, Bakst was mainly a painter of monumental compositions and numerous portraits drawn in precise line and demonstrating a fine perception of the individual. He also designed and arranged painting displays. He won fame, however, above all in theatrical work as the designer of stage sets and costumes for the Ballets Russes.

171. Portrait of Levitan, 1899 (cat. 200).

GELA SEKSZTAJN
b. Warsaw, 1907; d. Treblinka, 1943
Painter.
Studied at the Academy of Fine Arts in Cracow (1924).
Her media were watercolours and drawing. She produced mainly still-lifes and portraits, in particular children's likenesses.
During the war she took an active part in the artistic life of the Warsaw ghetto. Some of her drawings and watercolours
have survived in the Ringelblum Archives – mostly works produced before the war and in the ghetto.

172. Self-portrait (cat. 201).

JÓZEF ŚLIWNIAK

b. Kiev, 1899; d. Treblinka, 1942

Metalwork artist, graphic artist, stage designer, member of the Group of Seven.

No information on the course of his studies.

Śliwniak engaged mainly in metalwork. He created portraits and figural compositions (*Water Carrier, The Whore of Babylon*) rendered in soft, rounded forms of flowing fine contours, with the silhouettes and faces of the sitters merely outlined. Śliwniak also designed sets for Warsaw theatres and revues, such as "Skala" and "Azazel".

173. Head of a Woman (cat. 202).
174. **Marek Szwarc** Portrait of Bergelson, 1925 (cat. 203).

HENRYK (HENOCH) BARCIŃSKI

b. Łódź, 1896; d. ?, 1941

Painter, graphic artist, member of the Yung Yiddish and Dresdner Sezession.

Studied in Kacenbogen's school in Łódź; under Glicenstein in Warsaw (1915–16); and at the Academy of Fine Arts in Dresden (1919–26) under C. Gussman and R. Starel.

For many years Barciński remained under the influence of Expressionism. Realistic methods of composition and post-impressionist colour schemes appeared in his later works, in his landscapes of France and Spain.

175. John the Baptist, 1919
     (cat. 204).

גשוױדמעט משה פראדעערזאן.

חנוך בארצינסקי

„יוחנן המטביל"

176. **Wilhelm Wachtel** Christ in the Pogrom District, plate from the graphic series *Farewell to Galus* (cat. 205).

HENRYK KUNA

b. Warsaw, 1885 (1879); d. Toruń, 1945

Sculptor, painter, one of the founders of the "Rytm" Association of Polish Artists.

Studied in P. Weloński's studio and the Academy of Fine Arts in Cracow (1902–04) under K. Laszczka.

Kuna came from a very religious Jewish family. When he resolved to be a sculptor, he had to overcome not only his own doubts, but also the resistance of his milieu.

In his early works Kuna shows the influence of Auguste Rodin's impressionist sculpture. In c. 1910, fascinated with Aristide Maillol's art, he started introducing classicist elements. In the 1930's he turned to portrait sculpture He produced likenesses of many prominent men (e.g. K. Witkowski and T. Zieliński, 1933), as well as of women, the latter however inferior to his male heads as regards characterization.

177. Bust of Felicja Winawerowa (cat. 206).

KONSTANTY LASZCZKA
b. Riga, 1865; d. Cracow, 1956
Sculptor, ceramic artist, painter, graphic artist, member of the "Sztuka" Association of Artists, the "Sztuka Rodzima"
Society of Painters and Sculptors, Societé Nationale des Beaux-Arts, "Sztuka Stosowana" Society, Wiener Sezession, and
"Sculpture".
Studied in Jan Kryński's private school of sculpture in Warsaw (from 1885); with L. Pyrowicz (1889); in Paris in the Académie Julian (1891–92) with A. Mercié, and the Ecole Nationale et Speciale des Beaux-Arts (1892–96) with A. Falguière
and J. L. Gérôme.
Laszczka was a versatile artist, both as regards subject matter and formal devices. His style evolved from realism moving
through Impressionism to Art Nouveau stylization and Symbolism. He produced monumental sculptures, genre and symbolic
scenes, and worked in applied ceramic art.

178. Head of a Jew (cat. 207).

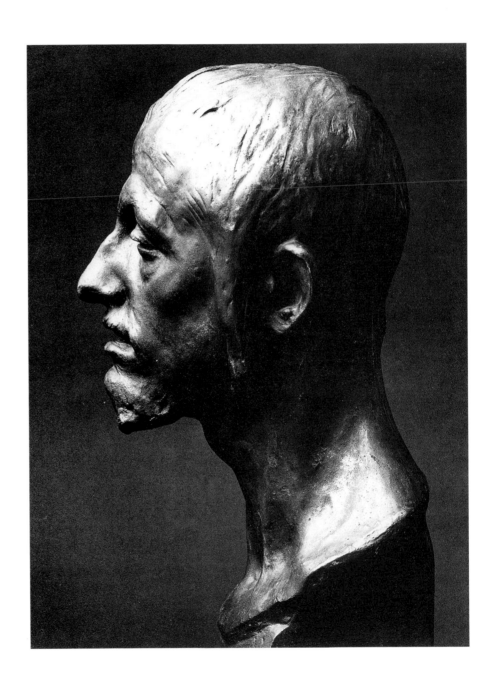

RYSZARD MOSZKOWSKI
b. Liège, 1906; d. Warsaw, 1945
Sculptor, architect, art critic. Studied at the Technical University in Liège; the Academy of Fine Arts in Ghent (1936–1937); and in Paris under A. Bourdelle and A. Maillot (1937).
Very little is known about his architectural designs. His sculptures are calm and static, clearly outlined masses. The method of composition is more expressive – rough, furrowed texture produces interesting pictorial effects. In some sculptures the coarse texture of hair contrasts with the smooth, polished faces (*Girl with a Plait*). He produced small, attractive idealized heads of girls and women as well as realistic male portraits.

179. Portrait of a woman with a shawl on her head (cat. 209).

180. Nude Boy, 1943 (cat. 208).

JULIA RINGEL-KEILOWA

b. Stryj, 1902; d. Warsaw, 1943

Sculptor, metalwork artist, member of the "Blok" Union of Polish Artists and the "Forma" Sculpture Cooperative. Studied philosophy and attended the Art College in Warsaw (1925–31) studying with T. Breyer and K. Stryjeński. Ringel-Keilowa sculpted mostly portraits, preferably in wood (*Nina*, 1935, *Statue of the Actress Elżbieta Barszczewska*, 1937), more rarely in marble, plaster or copperplate (*Small Head*). Her works have compact classicist forms recalling contemporary French sculpture and the work of Henryk Kuna. She also produced objects of utility in metal: tableware, cups, cutlery, lamps, candleholders, etc.

181. Statue of the Actress Elżbieta Barszczewska, 1937 (cat. 210).
182. Motherhood, c. 1937 (cat. 211).

HELENA GŁOGOWSKA
b. Zgierz, 1893
Sculptor. Studied in Paris (from 1911) at the faculty of literature of the Sorbonne, the Académie Colarossi, the Académie de la Grande Chaumière with A. Bourdelle; and the Art College in Warsaw (from 1923) under T. Breyer and S. Noakowski. Left Poland for Paris in 1939 and settled in São Paulo in 1940.
Głogowska was interested in various materials and produced works in bronze and wood, mostly studies of the human form. After the war she also engaged in ceramic work.

MAGDALENA GROSS
b. Warsaw, 1891; d. Warsaw, 1948
Sculptor.
Studied at the Art College in Warsaw under T. Breyer and H. Kuna, and for two years in Florence under F. Simi.
Gross's sculptures were usually small, unassuming works, for example portraits of Fryderyk Jarosy, Franc Fiszer, Leon Okręt, Stanisław Staszic and Dr. Tonchu-Ru, as well as images of animals. At first she sculpted birds: *Heron, Flamingo, Crowned Crane,* and from 1934 onwards also animals, e.g. *Little Llama, Aurochs, Elk.*

183. Head of a Woman (cat. 212).

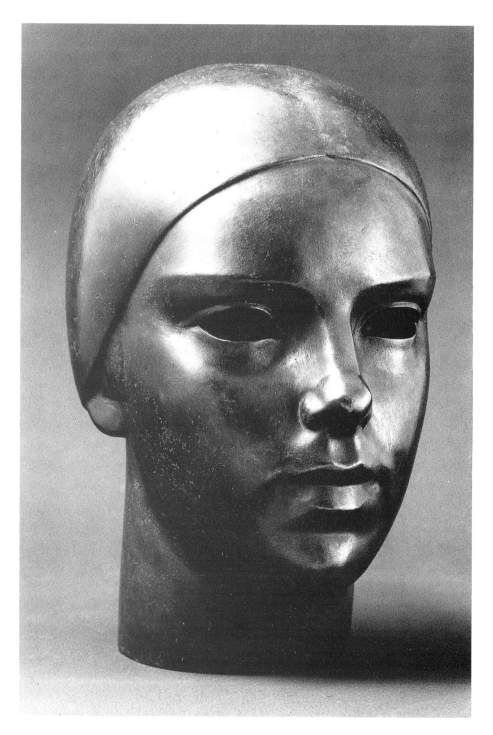

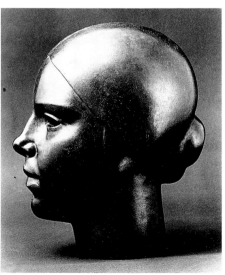

184. **Roman Kramsztyk** Head of a Girl Wearing a Turban (cat. 213).

185. **Gela Seksztajn** Portrait of a girl
(cat. 214).
186. Ghetto Jew, 1942 (cat. 215).

HERSZ SCHILIS (SZYLIS)
b. Łódź, 1909; d. Israel, 1987
Paiter, draughtsman.
Studied in Łódź, Warsaw and Munich.
Schilis is the author of numerous pictures on the subject of life in the ghetto, some of them produced during the war and constituting an impressive and moving document of those times.

MACIEJ LACHUR
b. Zagórze, 1927
Painter.
Studied for two years at the Academy of Fine Arts in Cracow.
In his work the theme of martyrdom is frequently present, e.g. in a series like *Ghetto, Ghetto Boy* and *Homeless Woman*.

187. Execution, 1957 (cat. 216).

MAREK OBERLÄNDER
b. Szczerzec near Lvov, 1922; d. Nice, 1978
Painter, graphic artist, draughtsman. Studied at the Academy of Fine Arts in Warsaw under T. Kulisiewicz.
Oberländer made his début at the famous exhibition of young Polish artists in Warsaw's Arsenal in 1955. In his works from this period – *The Stigmatized, Kol Nidre* – simplification, formal asceticism, expressive realism, a vivid and often brutal texture and sharp contrasts of value and colour served "to express the inexpressible pain of a Jew who had been miraculously saved from annihilation" (Zieliński). In the images of the *Hunchback* produced in 1957–58 the artist gradually departed from the literal depiction of man. He concentrated on rendering one chosen feature, or the figure's mental state. In the following years the consistent simplification of human form gradually turns a figure, into an organic smooth shape (series *Figures* and *Silhouettes*).
From 1966 on he painted exclusively landscape studies and musical impressions. Art for him became peace, joy, a form of therapy after several heart attacks.

188. Kol Nidre, 1955 (cat. 217).

HELENA GAŁKOWSKA
b. Morawica near Cracow, 1911
Tapestry designer.
Studied at the Academy of Fine Arts in Warsaw (1934–37) under M. Kotarbiński and W. Jastrzębowski. Her work should be treated together with the activity of her husband, Stefan Gałkowski. The two artists often worked together and together searched for new materials and artistic devices. Gałkowska's tapestries, which I. Huml described as "concretized painting", display enormous merits as regards composition and colour scheme.

189. Candleholder , 1978 (cat. 218).